STILL MEMORIES

JOHN MILLS

HUTCHINSON
LONDON

STILL MEMORIES

First published in the United Kingdom in 2000 by Hutchinson

The Random House Group Limited, 20 Vauxhall Bridge Road, London SW1V 2SA

Random House Australia (Pty) Limited, 20 Alfred Street, Milsons Point, Sydney, New South Wales 2061, Australia

Random House New Zealand Limited, 18 Poland Road, Glenfield, Auckland 10, New Zealand

Random House (Pty) Limited, Endulini, 5a Jubilee Road, Parktown 2193, South Africa

The Random House Group Limited Reg. No. 954009
www.randomhouse.co.uk

A CIP catalogue record for this book is available
from the British Library

Papers used by Random House
are natural, recyclable products made from wood grown in
sustainable forests. The manufacturing processes conform to
the environmental regulations of the country of origin

ISBN 0 09 179391 2

Designed by Anthony Cohen

Printed and bound in Great Britain by Butler & Tanner

CONTENTS

Introduction by Jonathan Mills

L EWIS ERNEST WATTS MILLS was born on February 22nd, 1908 at the Watts Naval training academy in Norfolk. When he was twelve years old his father, Lewis Mills, gave him his first camera, a Kodak Box Brownie, and they went down to the beach at Great Yarmouth to take his first photograph. It was September 21st, 1920. 79 years later he is still taking pictures.

STILL MEMORIES is, first of all, an intimate look at his family, his wife Mary Hayley Bell and his three children, Juliet, Hayley and myself. Second of all it is a testament to his art as a photographer. If he hadn't been an actor it is quite obvious that he could have made a successful career as a cameraman. Thirdly STILL MEMORIES is the extraordinary record of a man's life and career during the golden age of the cinema and theatre. All of this made all the more poignant due to the near total of his eyesight in the last two years.

Rarely has a man had a life so full of photographic memories, a life so rewarding, with close friends such as Noel Coward, Laurence Olivier, Vivien Leigh, Rex Harrison, David Niven, James Mason, Frank Sinatra, David Lean, Walt Disney, Douglas Fairbanks, Errol Flynn, Montgomery Clift, Richard Attenborough, Danny Kaye, Bob Hope, Tyrone Power, John Gielgud, the list goes on and on.

Many of the following photographs were thought to have been lost over the years. However, earlier this year, I discovered a cache of over 5000 transparencies in two mouse-eaten boxes in an unused corner of the attic of my parents' home in Denham Village. During the next two weeks I collected together more than 10,000 transparencies, stereo slides, prints and negatives. The stereo slides were found in a shoe box under the attic water tank and sadly many were damaged. These slides in their 3D stereo format were so breathtakingly beautiful that for a week I carried the viewer and the slides around with me in my briefcase, fearful they would disappear again. Only 350 survived.

These are rare images, moments in time. Quite simply an incredible journey across the 20th century.

Enjoy and Godspeed.

Jonathan Mills, White Horse Yard, Hampton
February 22, 1999

Foreword by Lord Attenborough

John Mills and Richard Attenborough *1956, 'Baby and the Battleship'*

JOHNNIE MILLS IS UNIQUE. The word is, I fear, somewhat overworked, but in this instance I believe it to be more than fully justified.

Although John Mills began his career in the theatre in 1929, it was through cinema that he became a household name. Incredible though it may seem, he was already one of Britain's very first movie stars when he played the lead in such major movies as *Brown on Resolution* fully 65 years ago and, of course, he has remained a star ever since.

By the 1940s, his fame was such that he found it impossible to attend any showbiz event without police protection for fear of being mobbed. And, year after year, embodying all the characteristics which the British most admire in a screen hero, he was overwhelmingly voted our most popular male star.

He was, however, much more than just a popular name. His skill and devotion to films endowed both them and the craft of screen acting with a stature that, before his time, neither had possessed, and he soon came to be regarded around the world as the quintessential British leading man.

He never deserted the theatre, however, and also achieved enormous success on both sides of the Atlantic in such stage productions as *Cavalcade* and *Jill Darling* before the war, and in peacetime with *Of Mice and Men*, *Ross*, *Veterans* and *Separate Tables* together, of course, with the two remarkable plays written by his beloved wife, Mary – *Men in Shadow* and *Duet for Two Hands*.

For many years, we all lived in Richmond, Surrey – Johnnie and Mary on the Hill and Sheila and I on the Green, where we remain. Johnnie and Mary eventually left Richmond and, having moved around quite a bit, came to rest in Denham. It is indicative of their relationship that friends never talk of them singly but always run their two names together – Johnnie-and-Mary. Theirs is an extraordinarily successful and happy marriage with their three children, Juliet, Hayley and Jonathan making up a very remarkable trio of siblings.

I first met Juliet (Bunny), aged a few weeks, when she made her very early

7

professional debut in *In Which We Serve*.

However, it was Bags (Hayley) with whom I really became involved. Mary had written a ravishing story called *Whistle Down the Wind*, currently a hugely successful theatre musical.

The original was a phenomenal piece of creative writing which could well have been conceived for the cinema, and my partner, Bryan Forbes, and I asked Mary if we could try and turn it into a film. 'Certainly,' came her reply and so we engaged Willis Hall and Keith Waterhouse to write the script. As Bryan had contributed some additional writing, I suggested to Mary (Ginger) and Johnnie that he should direct it. This was to be Bryan's first film as a director and proved to be an enormous success. As everyone knows, Bags played the lead quite enchantingly. Indeed, I am not at all certain that it wasn't the best of all the films Bryan and I made together.

However, the point of recounting this 1960s collaboration is to illustrate the impact of the Family Mills. We made the picture outside Burnley in Lancashire and Mary and Johnnie were with us for a large part of the shooting schedule. Their unity with their daughter, granting her encouragement, guidance and support, whilst demonstrating their confidence in Bryan, the fledgling director, and in me, a novice producer, was an amazing feat of loyalty.

It was primarily Johnnie, with the agreement of Len Deighton, his partner in the project, who offered me my own first chance to direct. I thought he was barmy. The faith he demonstrated in me, matched always by Mary, resulted in one of the major turning points of my cinematic career. The film was *Oh! What a Lovely War*, in which, as everyone knows, Johnnie played the lead.

Johnnie and Mary are the best example of showbiz parents I have ever encountered – wise, utterly selfless in their devotion to their children and always prepared to sublimate their own lives and concerns in the cause of their offspring. They have been a shining example to all of us who have attempted to bring up a family in this perilous profession.

John Mills and Richard Attenborough *1969, Oh What a Lovely War*

But in writing this foreword, it is proper that I should finish by concentrating on John Mills, the film star. In movies such as *We Dive at Dawn, Scott of the Antarctic, Morning Departure, The Colditz Story* and *Tunes of Glory* he came to epitomise the stalwart British establishment figure, basking in upper deck superiority. He played those parts impeccably. However, I believe his Shorty Blake in *In Which We Serve* and his wonderful performance in *The Baby and the Battleship* – both decidedly lower deck characters - are equal measure of his invention. He is also a brilliant comedian.

I am aware that it was his extraordinary performance in *Ryan's Daughter* which won him his Oscar but, for me, he was even more entitled to such recognition for the performance I would choose to mention above all others - his unforgettable and utterly wonderful Willie Mossop in *Hobson's Choice*.

Johnnie Mills has become a role model for the generations of actors who attempt to follow him. His amazing talent apart, he is the total professional, always sublimely prepared on the first day of an engagement, word perfect, his characterisations rooted in careful research and his infallible actor's instinct. And, of course, he is never ever late – an attribute that many less punctual players would do well to emulate.

I have known him and worked with him for sixty years. His are the standards to which I have always aspired. He is a man of the greatest integrity who is devoted absolutely to his calling. I have valued his true friendship since we first met in 1942. He has graced British stage and screen all his working life and has made priceless contributions to movies I have directed. He is a courageous man of unfailing loyalty and blessed with an unbounded sense of honour.

This marvellous collection of photographs and stories will, I am certain, prove fascinating to fan and friend alike, none more so than I. I not only admire him profoundly, but love him dearly.

Richard Attenborough

Preface by John Mills

My first photograph album, *1920*

T HE FOLLOWING is a selection of photographs from my collection that began eighty years ago. I am now 92 and the new millennium marks my 71st professional year on the stage. Many of these photographs were thought to be lost, but my son Jonathan recently rescued them from oblivion. We now, somehow, have managed to assemble eight decades of memories.

Some of the pictures have been selected for pure photographic reasons and some for their stories and memories. My wife of 59 years, Mary Hayley Bell, also must take credit for many of the stills, especially when it came to the Rolleiflex. Also Jonathan started shooting at age 10 when I gave him his first Kodak on a trip to Australia.

Sadly, many of the people in this book have now moved on to better hunting grounds but, happily, I still have my photographs and my memories. These photographs, whether taken by myself, my family or given to me over the years, have become a wonderful personal album. I do hope you enjoy them.

John Mills, Hills House, Denham Village
February 2000

Me and Stephen Fry, *1999 Hills House, Denham*

FOR MARY

ACKNOWLEDGEMENTS

Sir John and the publisher would like to express their appreciation to the following for their assistance and/or permission to reproduce the photographs: Angus McBean, Doug McKenzie, Frank Connor, Friedman-Abeles, Juliet Mills Collection, Keith Waldegrave, Maxwell Caulfield, Molly Blake Collection, Molly Daubeney Collection, Noel Coward Collection, Really Useful Company, Jonathan Mills, Mary Hayley Bell. Every effort has been made to trace the copyright owners and Sir John and the publisher would like to apologise to any whose copyright has been infringed.

Research and special assistance: Jill Thomson.
Special thanks to my editor, Paul Sidey, The Raymond Mander and Joe Mitchenson Theatre Collection, the BBC, Pictorial Press, the BFI, and everyone who has helped with *Still Memories*.

THE 1900s

My parents, Early Schooldays in Suffolk and My First Theatrical Appearance.

'A Midsummer Night's Dream' *1918, Belton school, Belton, Suffolk*
I was ten years old when I first played Puck in school. My mother made the costume for me.

Walter Luck TUNBRIDGE WELLS.

Me *1908, Watts Naval Training College (above)*

My Mother and Father *1895, Suffolk (left)*

Watts Naval Training College *1908, Suffolk*

I was born at Watts Naval Training College and lived here until 1910.

Watts Naval Training College group *1910, Suffolk*
That's me top right being held by a teacher.

Belton Schoolhouse
1911, Belton, Suffolk
This was our home from 1910
to 1920.

Me (Third from right, front row) *1914, Belton School.*
My father was headmaster of Belton, I was always trying to get caned to show I was one of the boys. One day when he was reading the prayers, I sneaked out of the hall, climbed onto the roof and then rang the bell. He gave me a terrific bollocking but I never got caned in front of the school. I was vastly disappointed.

Annette Mills *1914, Madame Baird's Academy of Dance*

This is my sister Annie at Madame Baird's Academy of Dance. It was wartime, 1914. Annie was 18 and fell madly in love with a good-looking Lieutenant called McKlenaghan and he went off to the Somme. At that time, the life expectancy of a 1st Lieutenant was under six weeks.

He had been at the front for not more than four or five months when he was severely wounded and was taken by car to a hospital in Paris. Annie was informed and somehow got out there. He died in her arms about two hours later.

I remember when the big Zeppelin was shot down in flames over the sea at Yarmouth. It was only a few miles from Belton. Streams of people in their night-gowns were walking around in shock because they'd never seen anything like it.

Colonel Francis Hayley Bell
1917, London

Mary's father was Colonel Francis Hayley Bell, multi-decorated veteran of the Boer and First World wars. He fought in a total of five wars. He loved being a soldier. He later became Commissioner of Shanghai, but had to leave China after twenty years when the Japanese/Chinese war broke out. Around this time he lost his quite considerable fortune in roubles when revolution changed Russia for ever. He also was one of three partners who came up with the idea for 'cat's eye' road lights and then was cheated out of his share. He died in 1945 of gangrene from an old First World War wound.

Me as Puck *1918, Belton, Suffolk (left)*

St Paul's Choir Audition *1918, London*

My parents tried to get me a scholarship at St Paul's, London. In those days one way of doing it was to be taken in for the choir. Even for the audition, you had to be dressed in a mortarboard and Eton suit. I missed it by one place.

THE 1920s

Teenage years in Belton and Great Yarmouth, Starting Work, My first Car, Amateur Dramatics, First experiments in Photography

My Father, Auntie Jim and Molly (Buddy) *1922, The Serpentine, Hyde Park, London.*

It was always a great treat to go to London and go rowing on the Serpentine. Dads loved any kind of boat.

Mums *1920, Belton, Suffolk*

My next photograph was of my mother sitting beside the fire in the schoolhouse in Belton. There was a large mirror above the mantelpiece and, when we developed the picture, my father said, 'There is something in the corner of the mirror, what is it?' When we printed it, we saw it was a reflection of me taking the photograph. From then on I was hooked.

Dads *1920, Great Yarmouth Beach, Suffolk*

I became captivated by photography when I was young, having watched my father developing film. It was my father's hobby and he was very good at it. He had a darkroom in the village schoolhouse in Belton. When the images magically came to life, we hung the pictures up to dry, then printed them in the sun… This photograph of my father was my very first. He gave me a Kodak Box Brownie and we went down to the beach at Great Yarmouth. I got him to lean against the boat with his legs crossed. He had a long raincoat and a trilby on. Odd clothes for the beach.

Me, on the rocks *1920, Sherringham, Suffolk*

Molly (Buddy) and Aunt Rosa *1922, Oxford Gardens, London*

I took this shot outside Madame Baird's house in Oxford Gardens. This is where my sister, Annie, took dancing lessons and also where my mother worked as cook/housekeeper to supplement the family fortunes. It was also the first place I saw a French letter, which had landed in the flower box outside the living room window. I thought it was a balloon and was in the process of blowing it up when my mother walked into the room and snatched it out of my hand. In those days, French letters were unmentionable!

John, Bree, Smith and Ferley at Norwich High School Race
1921, Norfolk

I won the under-14 hundred yards dash and a toast rack. Everyone wanted me to run the quarter mile but I wanted to save myself for the hundred yards so I could win the toast rack for my mother. I'm third from the right. Note that everyone is looking at the camera.

Four of my friends on Sports Day *(left)*

The cast of 'As You Like It' 1922, Norwich High School, Norfolk

Norwich High School Football XI, *1923, Norfolk*

It was a really good team that year and I was selected with George Rope for a try-out with Norwich City.
He was three stones heavier and got selected. I was told to eat some rice pudding and come back next year.

Me and Auntie Lily
1924, Felixstowe, Suffolk

Five of 'em *1924, Felixstowe, Suffolk*

My mother with Auntie Rosa, Auntie Jimmy, Auntie Betty, Auntie Lily on Felixstowe beach in front of our hut. Every summer we rented a hut on the beach. It was a three-mile walk from our house.

Drink to me only with thine eyes *1924, Felixstowe, Suffolk*

Dads on 'The Belle' 1924, Great Yarmouth, Norfolk

My father loved *The Belle*. Occasionally, for a treat, we would take it from Great Yarmouth to Gorleston. Everyone would usually throw up except for Dads.

'The Belle' arriving at the pier
1923, Felixstowe, Suffolk

Me and Buddy swimming
1924, Felixstowe, Suffolk

Annette Mills and Robert Sielle *1925*

This is a photograph of Bobby and Annette when they first started dancing together. I remember them doing a wildly funny routine where they wore pads on their knees. The pads were made to look like shoes, they both wore long dresses and they did this hilarious `pas de deux' as two little Victorian ladies.

There were the Castles, The Astaires, and Sielle and Mills. Sielle's real name was C.L. Roberts. He was a pilot in WW1 and used to drop bombs by hand behind the German lines.

After a period in New York at the famous Ambassadeurs' Club, Sielle and Annette came back to England and brought the Charleston with them.

On one memorable occasion, they took me up to London when I was sixteen. All of a sudden I found myself in the West End in a hired dinner jacket at Cero's Club, which was the chic place to go, with this glorious sister of mine dancing with Bobby Sielle. I faded out at about midnight full of champagne. At that time everyone wore very stiff shirts. Mine went up under my chin and ended at my navel. Annette said, 'We'll take you up to bed, Johnny, and then we'll come up later and say goodnight.' When they found me, I was sitting on the bed, bolt upright. I'd fallen asleep on the starched shirt front.

Me and my father in the Morgan *1927, Suffolk*

This was my first car, a Morgan three-wheeler. I bought it while I was working in Ipswich at R.W. Paul Ltd., the well-known corn merchants. The car was always breaking down but I did drive it to Cornwall once with Vic Jennings. By the time I get home everything was tied up with string. The accelerator was on the steering wheel. It had a twin engine, and you had to crank start…Those were the days, when motoring was a real adventure. Once, the single wheel at the back got stuck in a tramline in Ipswich. I couldn't get it out and I ended up driving nearly all the way to the end of the line. I was terrified a tram was going to come and run me over.

Me *1928*

Although committed to working in the office in Ipswich, I still dreamed of becoming a professional actor. I paid for this first publicity still while I was in *A Paper Chase* and it appeared in the *Felixtowe Times*.

Me *1929*

Another shot taken by my sister, Annie, during the time I was a door-to-door salesman in London for Sanitas, a toilet paper company. After three years I left my job at the Corn Exchange in Ipswich determined to get into the theatre in London. It took many months, and I nearly starved in the process.

The cast of the Vicar's Amateur Dramatic Society in 'A Paper Chase' *1928, Ipswich*

While I was working in Ipswich, I joined the Vicar's Amateur Dramatic Society, VADS, after being refused by the Felixtowe Players. The vicar and his wife were very sweet and we did two productions in the church hall, my first role being the gardener in *A Paper Chase*.

Me rehearsing for 'Ready for the River' Cabaret *1929, London*

This shot was taken by my sister Annie on her balcony in Swiss Cottage while I was rehearsing a cabaret I did with George Posford. We were called Posford and Mills and opened the Mitre nightclub in Regent Street. Unfortunately, after ten minutes, a fight broke out which closed the club for good. So I opened and closed the club in one night.

Me and Dilla Dati *1927, Suffolk*

Dilla Dati was my greatest friend all the way through school. After we left, he used to come out in his father's car, an Ensaldo, and tow me home when the Morgan broke down. This was during the period when I was a travelling salesman, selling Sanitas toilet paper.

I also fell madly in love with his sister, Gina. Their parents owned a wonderful Italian restaurant in Soho where they would often give me a free meal while I stared at Gina.

Me in the chorus of '*The Five O'Clock Girl*' *1929 (2nd row third from left)*

My first real professional acting job was in the back row of the chorus at the London Hippodrome in *The Five O' Clock Girl*. When I walked on the stage, I knew I had come home. It was also the first time I became conscious of homosexuals. There were twenty-five chaps in the chorus, twenty of them that way inclined. I realised this when they would put on make-up to go out after the show!

THE 1930s

The Far East, Mary Hayley Bell (Leica very much), Musicals and Reviews, My first film part, In The Army

The cast of 'A Midsummer's Night Dream' - Me, Robert Helpmann, Ursula Jeans, Edward Chapman, Pamela Browne, George Browne, and Dorothy Hyson *1938, The Old Vic, London*

The Quaints: Peter Owen, Chubby Salew, Ronald Brantford, Bruce Carfax, James Grant Anderson (manager) and me
1929, Quetta

I joined The Quaints Company and toured around the Far East for fifteen months.

Noel Coward was on holiday in the Far East when he saw that a touring group called The Quaints was performing *Hamlet* that night. Amused at the idea, he went along to the evening show. As fate would have it, the actor who was playing Horatio got terribly drunk at the governor's lunch party so it was decided to perform *Mr. Cinders* instead. R.B. Salisbury was unable to play the lead, and I, as understudy, got the chance to play this great part in front of the Master. It was one of the most memorable nights of my life.

The following day Noel asked if he could play Stanhope in *Journey's End*. Naturally we all fell about. During my death scene as Raleigh, Noel leaned over me, and his heavy tin hat fell off his head and landed in my crotch, which brought me temporarily back to life with a terrible scream! Noel played Stanhope for four nights after only three days' rehearsal. He stayed with the company for the next five weeks.

I still remember his little song about the commissioner's wife whom he sat next to at lunch. Noel asked her if she enjoyed the theatre and she replied, 'Frankly I don't care about it much.'

Whoops lady Clemente
Not dulce but extremely fermiente
A little dull at 35
A bore at 44
You really are a fountainhead of fun in Singapore.

Me and Geoff Salisbury *1929, Port Said*

On the deck of 'The City of Lahore' on our way to India. Geoff was the son of the owner of The Quaints, R. B. Salisbury.

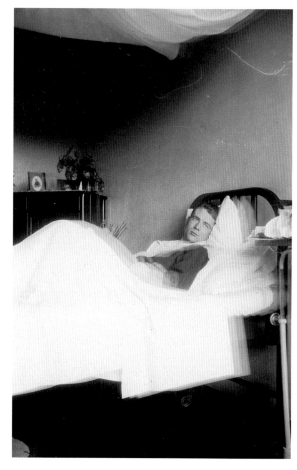

Me in hospital *1930, Shanghai*

I cut my finger on a rusty nail on the set of *Journey's End*. It became infected and I was rushed to hospital where, for three days, a Japanese doctor's treatment was to squeeze the hideously swollen finger with pliers till I passed out. I was rescued by my girlfriend, Aileen, who sneaked me out by the fire escape at night thereby saving my finger and possibly my hand.

Some of my shots of China

Me in 1930, *Shanghai, China*

The first time I met Mary Hayley Bell was at a tennis party given by her father for The Quaints. He was the Commissioner of Tientsin and she was the ballboy with flaming red hair.

Me as 'Charley's Aunt'
1930 New Theatre

Within two weeks of my return from India I auditioned for the title role in *Charley's Aunt*. At 22 I was the youngest to play the role. In this shot I had just returned from being flown around Blackpool tower five times for publicity.

The second time I played the part was in another production put on by Binkie Beaumont and the director was Johnny Gielgud. I remember particularly the last rehearsal at the Haymarket. It was summer, and blinding hot. We finished Act 1 and Johnny was in front, nobody else. Sweating, wig awry, I walked to the footlights and said, 'Johnny…are you there?' and a voice said, 'Yes.' I said, 'How was it?' and a voice came back: '*Interminable.*' We opened that night.

The Duke of York's Theatre *1931, London (left)*

I took this shot on May 1st 1931. *London Wall* was my first straight play in London. And there I am (above) with my co-starts, Helen Goss and Nadine March. I played an office boy and was quite a hit.

Charles B. Cochran *1931, London*

I auditioned for Cochran's 1931 Revue in front of the great man and, following my rendition of *Just a One Man Girl*, he took me in a taxi to The London Pavilion and offered me a contract for £15 a week. This was all organised by Noel Coward.

Mary Hayley Bell, Stella Patrick Campbell *1931, London*

These pictures of Mary on the roof of RADA rehearsing
Two Gentlemen of Verona were taken before I met her for
the second time. But I did see her in *Tony Draws a Horse*.
Marvellous. She was Lilian Braithwaite's understudy.
When Lilian, who at the time was a very big star, left,
Mary took over and was so good she stayed in the play
and eventually went to Broadway with it. This of course
was during the war. Very dodgy. Ships being blown up
left and right…Anyway, the play got a terrible notice
from someone called Luscious Bebe, (he was a big radio
critic). On the day it opened he declared that 'Tony
Draws a Blank!' The play came off after a few weeks but
someone at MGM had seen Mary's performance and
they offered her a seven-year deal in Hollywood. 'Great
eyes, great face but will need a nose job.' She didn't take
it. She came back to England, the war and me.

Will Fyffe and Bud Flanagan
'Give me a Ring', 1933, London Hippodrome

In 1933 there was a big musical, *Give Me a Ring*, running in London at the London Hippodrome. It starred the big stars of the time, Evelyn Laye, Flanagan and Allen and Will Fyffe. The leading juvenile, who had the numbers with Evelyn, had a problem with his passport and they gave him only a week to stay in England. George Black, who owned the theatre, rang me up and said, 'I'm in trouble because the man understudying is a very nice chap but he really shouldn't be on the stage and if he had to go on I really don't know what would happen. It's a lot to ask, you have three numbers with Evelyn Laye, you are the leading juvenile, you go right through the play and you have to go on in under

a week. Can you do it?' So of course, I said yes straight away. For a week I hardly went to bed, I learned the tap routines, I learned the dialogue, everything. The curtain went up on the first night and I knew it all but I wasn't quite sure where I went on and where I went off and Evelyn had to lead me through the whole thing. She got me through it.

Bud Flanagan and Chesney Allen were part of the Crazy Gang and notorious to work with. They were very naughty boys. One evening I was standing in the wings and Bud started talking to me and, while he was talking, he was tapping me on the chest. He was saying, 'Now you're only a youngster but I'll tell you, if you stay with it you're going to be a big star, there's no doubt.' And every time he spoke he tapped me on the chest. I said, 'Thanks, that's very nice of you.' Then my cue came and I went on. Evelyn was standing in the middle of the stage looking absolutely glorious and this was the big love duet which we all thought was rather sweet and corny. She started off with the verse and I was standing there gazing adoringly into her eyes and she suddenly looked down at my chest and started to giggle. She only just managed to get to the end of the verse. Before I started singing, I looked down and there were seven pieces of rather dirty chewing gum stuck on my shirtfront. I don't know how we managed to get through the number.

Bud always carried his famous walking stick and those were the days of fly buttons. Zips hadn't been heard of. We would always have a little chat before we went on and, at the right moment, Bud always managed to hook his stick into my flies so I either made an entrance sprawling onto the stage, or sidled on slowly with my back to the audience so I could do myself up. People came in just to see the entrances…

I remember another evening with Bud, where I had the big dramatic part and George Black was very, very keen on seeing it well acted. There was this scene set in the office, where I had to say, 'Now listen, I've had enough of this, I'm off. I'm leaving the firm, I haven't got much money but I'm going.' I picked my trilby hat up with a flourish and out of it flew an egg which splattered on the stage all over Debroy Summers, the famous conductor. I was playing opposite a man called Aubrey Dexter, who was a notorious giggler. We were having a bit of a problem anyway before the egg incident. His first line never came out and my next one didn't either. For about three or four minutes we were helpless with laughter, although I'm not sure the audience even saw what happened with the egg, it was so quick. But a message came round later,

'Would Mr. Mills and Mr. Dexter please see Mr. Black in the theatre tomorrow morning at 11 0'clock.' This was the first time I'd starred in a big musical, and with Evelyn Laye. Aubrey and I both thought we were for the chop. So next day we were ready for the worst.

George said, 'I saw the show last night. It wasn't very good. That was my favourite scene in the show. It's quite disgraceful, neither of you could speak, the audience didn't know what was going on and that's not good enough.' Right we thought, here we go. Then he said, 'What I want you to do is play the scene for me. Properly.' After the first line we started to giggle. In the certain knowledge that we were about to get the sack, we laughed for about five minutes like hysterical schoolgirls. He looked at us balefully. 'Now have you finished?' he said. 'Yes Mr. Black,' we replied. 'OK,' he said, 'don't do it again.' He was one of the great men in the theatre. We stayed in the show and it ran for a year.

Me and Jessie Mathews *1932, 'The Midshipmaid'*

I was playing in *Words and Music* when a talent scout from Gaumont British came to the play. In the dressing room afterwards I was offered the part of Midshipman Golightly opposite Jessie Matthews. This was my first film role. I was playing in *Words and Music* in the evening and filming during the day.

Me in '*Those Were the Days*' *1934*

Me and Kay Hammond *1933*

Britannia of Billingsgate was another Gaumont British picture with Gordon Harker as the star.

**Me, Louise Brown, Frances Day, Arthur Driscoe
and cast of '*Jill Darling*'** *1934, London*

A marvellous still from *Jill Darling*. In the show I
sang 'I'm on a Seesaw' with Louise Brown, which
I am still singing today in cabaret, 64 years later!
I fell head over heels for Louise. This musical was
a big break for me. I was the leading man and
had all the numbers with both Louise and
Frances.

I first met Frances at Zelia Ray's dance academy
in 1928. We did our first audition together
calling ourselves Mills and Day at The New Cross
Empire. It was a terrible place. If the audience
didn't like what they saw they'd throw thing at
you. But Frances had this amazing chest and a
bulldog who lifted his leg on the footlights. We
survived.

Frances Day was the original 'femme fatale'. I
saw danger lights flashing everywhere.

Me *'Brown on Resolution' 1935, London (left)*

Walter Forde directed *Brown on Resolution*. I went for the main part, but I was told I didn't look enough like a sailor. The next day, I borrowed a sailor's uniform, went back and got the job. This was the film that made me what is called 'a star'.

In one scene I had been captured with Jimmy Hanley. We were on this German cruiser and I had planned an escape. It was to take place at night. I was to steal a rifle, creep along the deck with my boots round my neck, jump from the deck of the cruiser into the sea and swim to Resolution Island. The director asked, 'Can you do this yourself?'

In those days I did all of the stunts myself. 'Don't you worry,' I replied. 'I'll manage.'

It was a horrifying drop, miles down. They had a big circle of boats with searchlights on and I was to land in the middle. I didn't like the look of it at all. One of the Petty officers saw my expression. There was some time to kill and I was already losing my nerve. 'Blimey,' he said. 'You had better come down to the mess with me and have a drink with the boys.' An hour later I'd had three very large navy rums. They are very sweet and taste like something you might get in the nursery. I was plastered, but happy as a sandboy. I could have jumped off the Eiffel Tower. It was all to be in one shot, no cuts.

When they said 'Action' I tottered out on deck, and dropped overboard like a sack of potatoes. It seemed ten years before I hit the water, but I was fine and I could have swum to Resolution Island and back!

Me and Lilli Palmer *1936, 'First Offence'*

This is a still of me and a very beautiful German girl called Lilli Palmer. She was just starting out on a very illustrious career, and she was a knockout. Paris was one of our favourite haunts and we had a number of friends there.

One night we went out and had dinner at Montmartre and emptied the cellars. In the morning I was supposed to be shooting in a swimming pool and was due on the set at 7.30. I arrived, feeling absolutely dreadful, head throbbing, mouth dry, decidedly queasy.

The director said, 'Now this is quite a simple shot, you dive into the deep end and halfway down the pool you rescue Lilli. She is in trouble and you haul her out. That's all there is to it.' Out of the corner of my eye I saw something floating on the surface. 'What's that?' I said. It was the body of a man with a totally white face and staring eyes. He was dead. No two ways about it.

It was some time later before we were able to do the scene. How I got in the water, God knows…There was a very strong smell of disinfectant. But, apart from this grisly incident, the picture was great fun and one of those I could quite easily forget.

STRAND THEATRE W.C.2

ROBERTSON HARE
ALFRED DRAYTON
JOHN MILLS

LONDON'S LOUDEST & LONGEST LAUGH

AREN'T MEN BEASTS!

By VERNON SYLVAINE

Me, Robertson Hare and Alfred Drayton
1936, Strand Theatre, London

Another double job. I was playing in *Aren't Men Beasts* at night at The Strand Theatre which ran for a year with two of the greatest farce actors alive – Robertson 'Bunny' Hare and Alfred Drayton. When the curtain came down, I would be driven to Wiltshire where I was doing a film. This meant getting up at 4.30am, shooting until 4pm then taking the car back to London for my evening performance. It was all go.

Bunny Hare was tiny, very funny and extraordinary-looking. The play was directed by another very funny, marvellous actor called Leslie Henderson, whose directorial advice was quite succinct: 'I want you to form a line, face the front and bark into the abyss.' It was all great fun.

There was one occasion during a matinée when we were standing in this line barking into the abyss and Bunny had one famous word, 'indubitably'. Which he delivered inimitably. At the same time, he jumped up in the air and let rip the largest fart you have ever heard in your life – loud enough for the audience to hear. We couldn't stop laughing, except for Alfred Drayton. The farce was *Hamlet* to him.

The next night we had pulled ourselves together and tried the scene again. At a certain moment Alfred had to say, 'Shut up!' He only got as far as, 'Shut…' when the top set of his false teeth flew out. Somehow he grabbed them in mid air, turned his back, put his teeth in and then went on talking. But Bunny and I were incapable of saying another word. God knows what the audience made of it.

Yvonne André and Helene Larah *1936*

Helene Larah played Clare, the French girl, and true to form, I fell madly in love with her and arranged an illicit weekend in Blackpool. Things didn't work out. We used 1914 uniforms in the play which had obviously not been to the cleaners, and on the Friday night. I felt a terrible irritation. I couldn't believe this terrible thing was happening to me so I took four of the culprits in a matchbox to the chemist and said, 'What are these?' And he said, 'Crabs of course.' I took my courage in both hands and explained the dilemma to Helene. She looked at me and said, 'Oh, you have papillons d'amour.' I said, 'That is a much more attractive name for them, but yes!' We consequently had a wonderful weekend. Vive la France! A curious footnote to this story is that Mary originally auditioned for the part of the French girl.

Me and Francis Day *1937 'Floodlight'*

This revue was written by Beverly Nichols and reunited me with Frances Day. The critics weren't kind and we closed after a short run. Frances by this time had blossomed into one of the most fascinating characters in musical theatre. I'll never forget a wonderful holiday after the play closed on a yacht Frances borrowed. Tony Pélissier, Isador Kerman and I were her guests on a trip to Deauville.

Me and Ursula Jeans *1939, 'She Stoops to Conquer', Old Vic Theatre, London*

'The Pelisssier Follies of 1938'
London

The Pélissier Follies of 1938 was written by my great friend, Tony Pélissier (at the back, centre in suit). His father wrote the original follies during WW1.

Mary Haley Bell *1938, 'Radio Pictorial', Sydney, Australia*

Mary Haley Bell *1938*

This is the extraordinary costume Mary was wearing when she asked me for an autograph in aid of the Actors' Orphanage. She was doing a sketch for Ivor Novello. She paid me sixpence for my signature, which was the going rate.

Anthony Pélissier, who produced '*The Pélissier Follies of 1938*', had invited me to a party one evening, saying it was very important I should be there. He knew I was rehearsing at night but insisted that he had a present to give me. It was at his mother's (Fay Compton) flat in Dorset Square. I turned up on the dot and said, 'OK, Tony, I haven't got long unfortunately. Where's my present?' He replied, 'I haven't got it at the moment. It isn't here. Something has gone wrong.'

After about twenty minutes I decided it was time to go. As I got to the lift, the door opened and a very beautiful young girl, with flaming red hair, stepped out. I said, 'Hello,' and she said, 'Hello…You don't remember me do you?' I said, ' Yes I do, your name is Mary Hayley Bell and I met you in Tientsin, China, and your father is Colonel Hayley Bell.' And I offered to escort her down the corridor and back to the party.

Tony looked delighted to see us. I said, 'No sign of my present, is there?' He said, 'As a matter of fact, there is.' And pointed at Mary. Tony knew I had been going through a bad time in the love department, and Mary had had the same trouble. She'd had just finished an affair in Australia with a wretched man who had come back to England and married someone else. She and I were both in a bit of a state. But thanks to Tony, we've never looked back.

Me and Robert Helpmann 1938, 'A Midsummer's Night Dream',
The Old Vic, London

I was dining with the Oliviers one night at their sweet little place, Durham Cottage, in London. Having been in musicals for a few years and doing splendidly, I suddenly had this urge to become a straight actor. I turned down two musicals and was becoming very hard up.

That evening Tyrone Guthrie came round after rehearsals for *A Midsummer's Night Dream* to have a drink and a chat and I asked him how it was all going. 'All right, but I'm having a slight problem. I've got very good people in it but I cannot cast Puck.' Larry pointed to me and said, 'There he is.' Ty said, 'I can't offer it to Johnnie, he's earning £175 a week,' which was a fortune in those days. 'I can only pay £15.' I said I would be happy to play the part, that I would love to do it in fact. I said, 'I'll come to the Vic right now!'

Dorothy Hyson was in the cast playing Titania and it was a tremendous production, one of Guthrie's best. All the fairies had little electric lights which looked like candles. Halfway through dress rehearsal, which was the first time we'd seen Dot Hyson dressed up as the Fairy Queen, Ty Guthrie turned to me and said, 'She's beautiful isn't she? Absolutely ravishing, so I suppose it doesn't really matter that she doesn't understand a bloody word she is saying.' I've never forgotten it. Ty organised the most magnificent entrance for her, through an avenue of fairies with their electric candles right down to the footlights, where Robert Helpmann (who played Oberon) was waiting, with me as Puck kneeling at his feet. But on the first night Dot Hyson got halfway down the ramp, tripped, did a somersault, and ended up on her bottom with her legs in the air, revealing a rather grubby pair of knickers. How we managed to go on I shall never know.

We had a tremendous summer run with the play, but it was extremely hot and the carefully painted stripey colours on my skin-tight costume started to run. One August matinée, Bobby Helpmann said, 'Johnnie you're beginning to look absolutely disgusting…I'm going to have to fix your crotch.' He came to my dressing room after the show, but I'd completely forgotten that I had two friends in the Corn trade out front in the audience, who'd promised to come round later. So there I was, standing on a chair, legs wide apart, with Robert kneeling between them, painting stripes with a make-up stick on my crotch when the door suddenly opened and the call boy said, 'This is Mr. and Mrs. Rawlings from Ipswich, sir.' Nobody knew what to say for a moment. Then I said, 'Hello, enjoy the show?'

Me in 'Of Mice and Men'
1939, London

Of Mice and Men was one of Steinbeck's greatest plays and playing George was a tremendous break. It opened at the Gate Theatre and then transferred to the Apollo, a good success that was rudely interrupted by Hitler in the summer. Clare Luce came over from the New York production to appear in it and Niall MacGinnis played Lennie, who was excellent and rather terrifying.

I joined the Royal Engineers later with Anthony Pélissier.

Mary, Janet Johnson (Lady Birkin) and Friend
1939, London

Mary joined the Ambulance Corps with her great friend Janet Johnson.

Me in The Royal Engineers
1939, Royston, Hertfordshire

This was my first week in the army under canvas at Royston as a sapper in the Royal Engineers. The pay was one shilling a day and the catering was frightful.

Mary joined the Ambulance Corps with her great friend, Janet Johnson. On one occasion, Mary stole an ambulance and came to Royston to see me. She crawled under the camp wire. I was on the roof of a hut, camouflaging, when I looked down and saw her standing there. To my horror, a sergeant appeared but luckily he was a chum, Sergeant White. He said, 'You two better get out of here, smartish.' We went down to Banyers Hotel in Royston where I blew my day's pay on a hot bath. We had a marvellous dinner together, which I will never forget.

Me and Mary
1939, Isle of Wight

Just before war was declared Mary and I spent a wonderful illicit weekend on Dr Deeter's boat on the Isle of Wight. We never did take the boat out to sea...

I took quite a few self-portrait shots and this was the best.

The following Monday we did our 'getting caught scene for the solicitors'. Very decent, in pyjamas and dressing gowns, Mary and I lay side by side on the large double bed. There was a knock on the door and this midshipman chap came in from the solicitors. He said, 'Good morning. Are you Mr. John Mills?' I said,' Yes.' 'Are you Miss Mary Haley Bell?' She said, 'Yes.' He said, ' You're in bed together.' I said, 'It looks like it.' He said, 'Naturally in bed together?' I said,' Yes.' He said, 'That's fine, thank you so much, good morning, good luck.' And off he went.

We had to go through this dreadful performance, because my first marriage had broken down irretrievably. Mary didn't want me going off to Brighton with some blonde, so we used Annie's flat in London.

THE 1940s

Me and Alec Guiness *1945, 'Great Expectations'*
It was Alec's first film. He was quite nervous but brilliant as Herbert Pocket.

John and Mary Mills *January 16th 1941, London*
I was on a 48-hour leave. I had the date of my marriage engraved on my Reverso watch, 16.1.41, which was quite unnecessary. I have never needed reminding of the most marvellous day of my life.

Me, Mary and Vivien Leigh *1941, London*
Our wedding reception.

Mary and Wyn *1941, London*

Mary and her sister Wyn in an air raid shelter. The general camaraderie during the Blitz was wonderful, even if it was a terrifying experience. Especially the buzz bombs.

WIng Commander Dennis Hayley Bell, Colonel Francis Hayley Bell and Agnes Hayley Bell *1941, Buckingham Palace, London*

On March 11th 1941, we all went to Buckingham Palace where Dennis received his DFC. He was flying Hurricanes in a night fighter squadron. They called themselves 'Dangerous Drivers'. Very brave man.

Mary, Wyn and Agnes Hayley Bell *1941*

Wyn was working for MI5. No-one ever knew what she was doing, top secret stuff. Their mother, Agnes, was a qualified nurse working with the St John's Ambulance Corps.

16 Old Barrack Yard
1941, London

16 Old Barrack Yard was our first home together. We paid 27s 6d a week for it.

During the height of the Blitz, when I was back on leave, we decided to blow everything and go to the Café de Paris. I was getting out of my uniform and into a dinner jacket when I suddenly said, 'Do you mind if we don't go out?' Mary said she wouldn't mind a bit, and would cook a rabbit stew instead. We then took Hamlet, our first spaniel dog, for a walk in Hyde Park.

As we were strolling beside the Serpentine around 8 o'clock a terrible bombardment started. We sat quietly under a tree and waited an hour for it to end. Next morning we heard on the radio that the Café de Paris had received a direct hit. Many people had been killed including Snake Hips Johnson and his band. The Alexandra Hotel also was hit next to Old Barrack Yard, breaking all the windows in our flat.

Me, Mary and Juliet at The Oast House *1941, Kent*

We rented The Oast House in Kent in the relative safety of the country. In November we were having lunch with Noel, Larry and Vivien when Noel said to Mary, 'Aren't you having a baby?' Mary said, 'Yes.' Noel said, 'When?' Mary said, 'Now!' I rushed her to the hospital then returned to Old Barrack Yard. An hour later a terrible blitz started and I was unable to get back to the hospital. Juliet was born that night in the middle of one of the worst air raids of the war.

'Old Bill and Son' *1941, Denham, Buckinghamshire (right and overleaf)*

On the set.

Me in 'Cottage to Let' *1941, London*

This was my first job after I was invalided out of the army with a bleeding ulcer. I played a German spy… which upset a lot of my fans.

Laurence Olivier and Vivien Leigh *1940, 'Romeo and Juliet'*

I first met Larry when he was doing Noel's *Private Lives* with Gertie Lawrence at the Phoenix theatre in 1930. We hit it off immediately and became great friends. He sent me this photo with a note about their run in *Romeo and Juliet* in New York. He had just had a huge success with *Wuthering Heights* and Vivien with *Gone With the Wind*. Every studio in Hollywood was trying to sign them for life. Instead they decided to produce, with their own money, *Romeo and Juliet*. After several performances, they were walking towards the theatre one late afternoon, and there was a whole line of people on the street outside. Larry said, 'Isn't that great? We've got a smash on our hands.' But when they reached the box office they saw everyone was queuing up to get their money back! The play came off in three weeks and they lost a fortune!

Me, Larry Olivier, David Niven and the girls *1942 (opposite)*

These shots were taken at Primula's house in Hampshire. Larry, David and I were known as 'The Three Musketeers'. I remember the second time I met Niven early in 1941. We were living at Misbourne cottage in Denham Village and one afternoon this soldier knocked at the door in full battle kit and wearing a gas mask. He tried to kid us that a giant gas bomb had been dropped on Gerrards Cross and that we had to run for our lives. He was hysterical, always doing stuff like that. He was one of my dearest friends. Sadly, Prim died playing 'sardines' in Hollywood in 1946. In this game, one person has to hide, then everyone else goes looking. As soon as you find someone, you have to hide with them. The more the merrier. Prim was the first to go, and she found a door that looked as if it should open into a cupboard. But instead it was the entrance to the cellar. She fell down the stairs head first, and died the same day in hospital. A ghastly, awful accident.

Lord Mountbatten
1942

Lord Mountbatten wrote all the captain's speeches in *In Which We Serve*. We saw a lot of him during the filming and he was absolutely charming and knew everyone, even by their nicknames.

One day I met him, by chance, outside the studio. 'Hello, Johnnie,' he said, 'How are you?' I said, 'I'm fine.' He said, 'You were a brown job weren't you?' I said, 'Yes, I was in the army, sir.' 'Well,' he said, 'I was certain you were in the navy because I don't think I've ever seen you out of naval uniform.' I said, 'Do you know, sir, I added it up the other day, and, on film anyway, I've spent five years in the navy.' He said, 'I'm going to put this right, I'm going to make you an honorary member of The Kelly ship's company.' (That's the famous destroyer that was sunk in the film.) He was as good as his word and, through the post a week later, from the coxswain came a Kelly tie, a badge for my blazer and a Kelly crest. The Kelly motto was, 'Keep on'. I hung the crest on the loo door. I thought it appropriate. And I wear the tie nearly every time I am on television, and I get at least two or three letters from the survivors of the ship's company saying how nice it is to see another member of The Kelly.

The Raft scene *1942, 'In Which We Serve' (opposite)*

Our ship had been sunk, and the survivors were clinging to Carley floats trying to avoid being machine-gunned by the Germans. This had to be done at Denham studios. We couldn't shoot in the Mediterranean because of the war. They built a huge tank of water, which, after six weeks of continuous use, was seriously filthy and stank to high heaven. We all dreaded going back in. And before the big raft scene no one wanted to make the first move. Then Noel came out of his dressing room and said, 'Come on you chaps, what are you doing? Let's go.' And dived in head first. He came up, covered in filthy diesel oil, and spluttered, 'Dysentery in every ripple.'

During the filming, I had to get shot in the arm while hanging onto a Carley float. In those days, special effects were not as advanced as they are now, and no one knew how to get this shot without seriously hurting me. So they went out to Denham and bought a gross of what, in those days, we used to delicately call French letters. They fitted them to hollow steel pipes, then blew in compressed air to explode them. I think I must be the only actor to have been shot in the arm by a contraceptive!

On those Carley floats you will see The Master, Noel Coward, Bernard Miles who became Lord Miles, Richard Attenborough who became Lord Attenborough, and an old actor called John Mills who, by some fluke and a great deal of luck, became Sir John Mills CBE.

Me, David Lean and Noel Coward
1942, 'In Which We Serve', Denham Studios

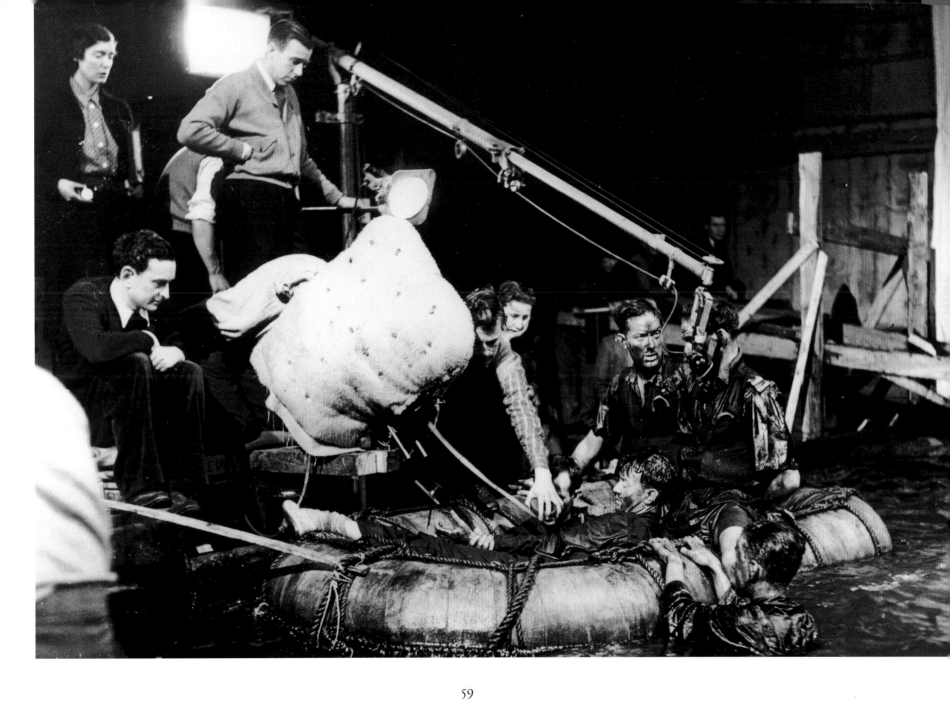

Me 'Men in Shadow' *1942,*
Vaudeville Theatre, London

Men in Shadow was Mary's
first play. It was originally
called *To Stall the Grey Rat*
but became *Men in Shadow*
after Noel read it and said
the play was good but the
title was 'piss poor'. I
directed it with Bernard
Miles and played the part of
Lew. It was a great success,
so much so that when Larry
called for tickets the day after we opened he couldn't get a seat. It ran
for nine months.

Richard Attenborough and Ronnie Waters *1943*

I had just been invalided out of the army, but was still in uniform,
when I was asked to go to the Arts Theatre in Cambridge to help with
the RAF production of *Men in Shadow*. I'd recently put it on in London
with a lot of actors from the army, navy and airforce, who weren't in the
best state of repair.

The first person I met was this young chap who looked about twelve
and a half, who was supposed to be playing my part. His name was
Attenborough. He was an air gunner, the stage manager told me, very
brave, especially as he felt airsick every time he went up. A big problem
when you have to wear an oxygen mask…

Before we had a run-through, I said to Attenborough, 'I have a
suggestion to make – go upstairs to your dressing room and make
yourself look a lot older, because anyone would think you're in the
nursery.' 'Yes sir,' he replied saluting smartly. He came down half an
hour later, plastered in make-up, looking like an Indian chief. That's
how I met Dickie. He was eighteen years old. Noel saw him in the play
and hired him immediately for a part in the film, *In Which We Serve*.

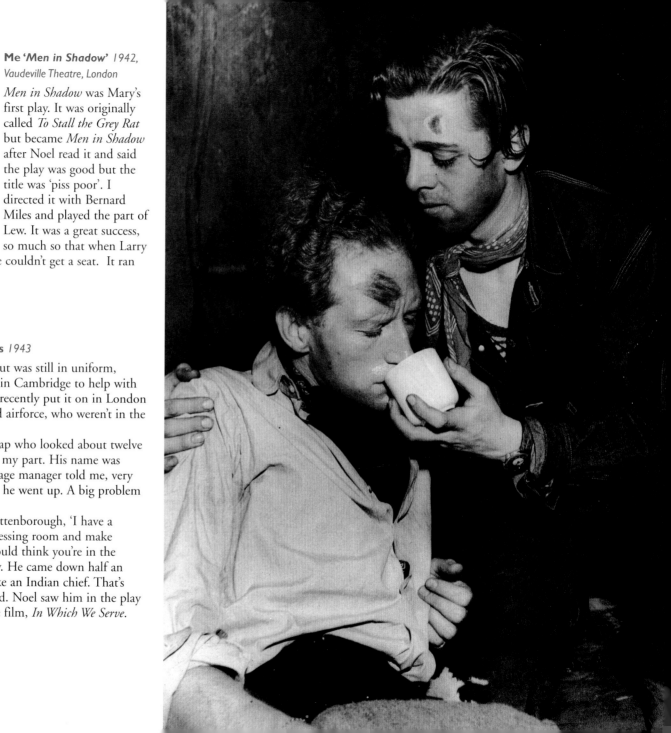

Misbourne Cottage *1944*

I bought Misbourne Cottage in Denham village in 1943 for £850 freehold. David Lean was also living in the village and quite nearby were Noel, David Niven and Ronnie Neame.

The girl with the moustache is Juliet

Laurence Olivier *1944 'Richard III', The Old Vic*

Larry gave me this wonderful still in 1944 during the Old Vic season at the New Theatre.

All good actors have their time and Larry then was at his peak. He was playing Richard III. It was a history-making company with Ralph Richardson, Alec Guinness and Peggy Ashcroft.

While we were getting ready for his first night, around 6 o'clock, the phone rang. It was Larry. The curtain was due to go up at 8 o'clock. He said, 'You're coming tonight aren't you?' 'Of course we're coming,' I said. 'What do you mean?' 'I want you to come and see me in my dressing room before the show,' he said. Nobody ever asks to see anybody before a show, not even your wife. I put down the telephone and said to Mary, 'What the hell is going on? It all sounds very strange.'

We got to the theatre at 7, an hour before the show and went up to the dressing room and there he was. He was prancing about in full make-up, false nose, hair, totally ready to go on. He said, 'Sit down I want to tell you something, you are my greatest friends and I want you to know that I'm in for a fucking awful flop.' He said, 'I'll tell you something. We haven't been through the play, John Burrell has cocked it up, I think. We are all over the shop, I don't know it, I've dried twice. I just want you to know that I know. That's all, see you later.'

So we tottered out, went to that pub across the road from the New Theatre and grabbed two double brandies. We thought we were in for a total disaster because he really meant it. Anyway, we were in the second row as the curtain went up and on came Larry. I cannot explain what it was like, it was a reincarnation of Edmund Kean who was supposed to have made ladies faint because he was so real. Larry gave the performance of his life. The cast was on the verge of hysteria, not sure what he was going to do and that gave an extra edge to the play as well. At the curtain call, the house went absolutely crazy. At supper afterwards, I told him it was the greatest performance that I had ever seen on the stage.

'How did you honestly feel?' I asked. He said, 'Well after "the winter of our discontent" for the first time in my life I felt I had the audience in the palm of my hand. It was a wonderful sensation. I became marvellously reckless. I knew, whatever I was doing, the audience was going to be with me.' During dinner I looked at him often and thought, I'm having dinner with Olivier. I'm bloody lucky to be with this great actor. He had such humility, and he was fantastic...

Larry, Mary and Vivien *1944*

Larry had just been made director of the Old Vic and was devastating everyone one with his performance of Richard III. I'll never forget that jacket.

Me and Robert Newton *1944, 'This Happy Breed', Denham Studios*

Robert Newton was offered Noel's part in the film, *This Happy Breed*. At the time, Newton was having a little trouble with the vino, so much so that in his contract it said he would forfeit his entire salary if he drank during filming. One Sunday, half the way through the shoot, I was mowing the lawn at Misbourne cottage when I saw what appeared to be a dirty-looking tramp swaying down the street towards me. When he got nearer I realised it was Bobby Newton, paralytic. Now David's house was only 100 yards away so I yanked Bobby into the cottage and Mary and I poured coffee and bacon and eggs into him. At one point he staggered out into the garden, took about two hundred pounds out of his pocket and threw it up into the air. Juliet was running all over the place trying to stop the money being blown into the river. Anyway we managed to sober him up and sneaked him out of the village. The next day I saw him in make-up and he looked like a ghost, awful. He turned to me and whispered, 'Now I know who my real friends are.'

Me *1944,*
'The Way to the Stars'

The director was a very good friend of mine, Puffin Asquith, with whom I had already made *We Dive at Dawn* and *A Cottage to Let*. I remember one very hot afternoon when I think Puffin had gone mad and had drunk a small lager for lunch. We were shooting the famous poem 'For Johnny' and he had worked out a long tracking shot which started way back and came in without a cut ending up in close-up...
'Do not despair for
Johnny head in air
He sleeps as sound as
Johnny underground
Fetch up no shroud for
Johnny in the cloud
But keep your tears for
him in after-years
Better by far for Johnny
the bright star
To keep your head and see
his children fed.'
I finished the line and there was dead silence. Puffin had built a little platform underneath the camera, and was sitting on it cross-legged like a little gnome and he'd gone to sleep. He woke up with a start and said, 'Oh...cut...wonderful.'

Me *1945, 'Duet for Two Hands', Lyric Theatre, London*
Me as Stephen Cass in Mary's second hit, *Duet for Two Hands.*

Me and David Lean *1945, 'Great Expectations'*

This was David Lean's first film as a director after co-directing *In Which We Serve* with Noel Coward. David always expected the actors to give a performance. He didn't have a very good reputation with actors and I believe he was happiest in the cutting room with the film in his hands.

**Finlay Curry
and Alec Guinness**
1945, 'Great Expectations' (above)

Me and Finlay Curry
1945, 'Great Expectations'

Finlay Curry was a great
character and very courageous.
We shot the paddle boat
sequence at night, the water
was freezing and it took forever.
I had to swim out and save
Finlay from the enormous
thrashing paddlewheel. Each
time more frightening. Finlay
got tremendous applause from
the crew. He was 82 years old.

'Great Expectations' (opposite)

These are the shots I took with
my Leica of the great fight scene
between the two convicts.

Me, Elspeth March and Jimmy Granger, 1946

Elspeth March and Jimmy (Stewart) Granger worked together in Aberdeen rep. In the same company were Dulcie Gray and Michael Dennison. This was just before the war. Mary had gone to Sherbourne School with Elspeth and they were great friends. I met Jimmy when we worked together in *Waterloo Road* where he played the villain.

'Great Expectations' 1946 (opposite)

Me, Juliet and Trevor Howard 1946, *'So Well Remembered'*
Juliet had a scene cutting a birthday cake.

Me and my father *1946, England (above)*
Celebrating Hayley's birth.

Hayley Mills christening *1946*
Hayley's christening with Martha Scott.

The Little House *1946 (opposite)*
I bought the Little House from Rex while I was working on *Great Expectations*. It was right on Denham golf course and, when I was working, I would jump over the fence and play 4 or 5 holes before going to the studio. I had a 12 handicap and was captain of the Stage Golfing Society.

Me, Mary and Haley *1947, England*

Mary *1947,*
The Queen Elizabeth

Mary arriving in New York.

Me, Mary, Rex And Lilli
1947, The Queen Elizabeth

This is the ship's photo on the Queen Elizabeth. By chance Rex and Lilli were travelling to Hollywood at the same time. The voyage was a riot, wonderful weather and the best suite on the ship, compliments of Mr. J Arthur Rank.

73

R.M.S. Queen Elizabeth
1947

I took this shot after we arrived in New York. It eventually won a photo contest in Beverly Hills.

Me and Lilli, Queen Elizabeth *1947 (left)*

Rex Harrison and me *1947, Hollywood*

Me, Douglas Fairbanks Jnr and Rex Harrison *1947, Hollywood*

It was a great time to be in Hollywood. All the great names were living there. I think every night we were invited to dinner with one legend or another. Spencer Tracy, Humphrey Bogart, Gary Cooper, Ronnie Coleman, Jimmy Cagney, Norma Shearer, Dougie Fairbanks, Bette Davis, they were all there.

Rex Harrison and friend *1947*

Me, Rex Harrison and girlfriend *1947, Hollywood*

There was usually one scandal or another in the news and while we were there one of Rex's ex girlfriends committed suicide. It was never made clear why but it was quite a story at the time.

Mary, *1947, Hollywood*

One of my all time favourites of Mary.

Me, Rex and Mary *1947, Hollywood*

Rex Harrison *1947, Hollywood*
Sexy Rexy. This was a shot from my first role of Kodachrome. Just fantastic color.

**Olivia de Havilland
and Jules Stein**
1947, Beverly Hills

I took these pictures at
Jules Stein's house in
Beverly Hills. He was head
of MCA and introduced
me to Lou Wasserman who
he said would represent
me. He was convinced that
one day Lou would one
day be one of the most
important men in
Hollywood. He was dead

Me and Mary *1947, Hollywood*

In 1947 I signed a five-year contract with the Rank Film Organization to
produce, direct and act. My first job was a wonderful working holiday in
America to publicise *Great Expectations*. It had already opened in America
and was a big hit. These are publicity shots from our whirlwind tour around
that amazing country. We ended up in Hollywood for a much needed two-
week holiday.

right. Olivia De Havilland was so beautiful that Mary was rather anxious that we
didn't stay too long at the lunch party.

Me *1947, 'Scott of the Antarctic', Norway*

On our return from Hollywood, I started work on *Scott of The Antarctic* in Norway. We took the boat, and it was a terribly rough crossing where the captain threw up during lunch.

In Finse where we filmed, all the blizzard and pony scenes we had to endure were real. It was so cold the camera operator got frostbite.

Montgomery Clift *1948 Switzerland*

Monty Clift was undoubtedly one of the great film actors. Became a very big star indeed. The first time we met him was on the slopes of St. Moritz. He happened to be in London around 1958 when Juliet was playing in *Five Finger Exercise*. She was sixteen years old and Monty was one of her great heroes. We had a flat in Green Street and Monty was coming along that evening to have dinner. He loved to drink and we were trying to be as careful as we could, keeping the cocktails away but we had some champagne and then he started on the vino and he was already well primed before he arrived. He didn't roll about, he didn't slur his words, he was apparently totally normal and quite charming. Juliet was starry-eyed and falling over backwards with excitement. Monty was chatting away about acting when he suddenly got up off the settee, for no reason at all, climbed up on the back, dived head first onto the floor and completely stunned himself. We gave him a glass of cold water and a cold wash and he became quite normal again. So, there we were, conversation was flourishing, Monty was sitting by the mantelpiece, talking to Juliet, when he stood up and toppled into the fire. I talked to him the next day and he didn't remember a thing about it. Needless to say, Juliet was still mad about him...

Errol aboard 'Zaca' *1948 Monte Carlo.*

Errol Flynn, Princess S and Sonny
1948 Switzerland and Monte Carlo.

Mary and I had a sort of routine. If I wasn't filming in January or February we would automatically take to the Alps. Either Austria, Switzerland or France. Whenever we could, we took the family and they became as mad about skiing as we were. One particular year we went to St. Moritz, which is one of my happy hunting grounds and I met up with a rather marvellous individual who at that time was a very big star indeed, Errol Flynn. Now I had heard a lot about Flynn. Some of it nice and some of it nasty, but I found him to be an absolute charmer.

Everyone recognised him in town, but he'd never skied in his life. So he enlisted the best Swiss guide available, who, incidentally, spoke hardly any English, and asked him to teach him. Of course this is one sport where, however hard you try, you can look ludicrous when you don't have the first idea what you are doing. Flynn would repeatedly fall on his arse in front of crowds of fans and his guide would bellow at him, 'Get up Mrs. Flynn! Mrs. Flynn you must lean forward, Mrs. Flynn you no good for the snow plough!' Errol took it wonderfully. He was a real card and we became great friends. When we went to America he invited us on board his black schooner with a crew of about six. He and Niven were great pals too, shared bachelor quarters in Hollywood. Sheer bedlam for the opposite sex!

Me and Arthur Rank *1948, Denham Studios*

On the set of *The History of Mr. Polly*, the first film I produced and starred in for my contract with The Rank Organisation. I knew Arthur well and we often used to go shooting together at the weekend. He came to me after *Great Expectations* and told me to write down what it would take for me to sign a five-year contract.

Jimmy McHugh was my agent at MCA at the time until he tried to attack his wife with an axe. Laurence Evans then became my agent and remained so for 40 years.

Although the film wasn't a great success, it remains one of my favourites.

Jean Simmons and Jimmy Granger
1948

Jimmy (Stewart) Granger fell in love with Jean Simmons, which ended his marriage to Elspeth March. In the spring of 1948 we drove to Portofino with them but, after a week, Jimmy became his usual tricky self and we had to leave with Jean in the back, sobbing all the way home.

Me, Juliet and Hayley *1949*

A fun shot of me and the girls.

Me, Mary, Noel, Larry and Vivien *1948, Northolt*

Mary and I, Noel and Larry and Viv all went to Paris for a long weekend, via Northolt airport. We had a wonderful time but we didn't see much of Noel as he spent it all in the Comédie Francaise. The rest of us went to all the great night clubs. I don't think we slept more that a couple of hours the whole weekend.

The Wick and Sussex House Farm, Hayley in Tiger Bay, Ice Cold in Alex, Dunkirk and Colditz, Disney and Hollywood

Me, Danny Kaye and Larry Olivier *1958, 'Night of a Hundred Stars' London Palladium*
We did Noel's number, *The Three Delinquents*. These shows were always so popular, we did them for a few years, wonderful fun.

Me, Mary, Larry and Lord Courtold Thompson *1950*

Larry, Douglas Fairbanks and Courts were Johnny's godparents. 'Courts' lived at Chequers where we often went and played bagatelle for hours. He left the marvellous house to the government.

I was in the Garrick Club, where I had been sent by Mary, when the doctor called with the news that I had a son. I was so happy I gave all the money in my pocket to the doorman as I rushed out of the club to the hospital. Mary had been terribly ill for months with asthma and our doctor had advised her against having the child. Mary was convinced it would be a red-headed boy and a marvellous doctor named Roy Saunders convinced us everything would be all right. And it was.

Jonathan was born on December 3rd 1949.

Opposite: **Me** *1950, 98 Cheyne Walk, London*

We were living at 98, Cheyne Walk when Jonathan was born. I painted the view often from the balcony overlooking the Thames.

After one long session I went inside and found myself covered in soot from the Battersea Power Station.

Mary, Noel, Joyce Carey and Graham Payne *1950 White Cliffs*

Unfortunately these Polaroid shots haven't aged well. We often went to Noel's house, *White Cliffs*, on St Margaret's Bay at the weekend. Wonderful times playing Scrabble or Canasta, which Noel was crazy about.

Richard Attenborough
1950, 'Morning Departure'

I was on location for *Morning Departure*, another picture Dickie Attenborough was in. We were at the Moonfleet Hotel near Weymouth in adjoining suites. I came into his room one night and, spread all over the bed, were enormous plans of a house. I said, 'What's this?' and Dickie said, 'It's a house called "The Old Friars" on Richmond Green. It's absolutely enormous, endless rooms and beautiful big garden…we're crazy even to be looking at it.' Then Sheila said, 'And look at that extra bit built on. There are eight rooms. What are we going to do with that?' And Dickie said, 'It could be offices.' Even in those days, he was looking ahead. He has been at 'Old Friars' ever since and they are now the offices of Beaver Films. He knew then exactly what he was up to and Mary and I always felt that his future was going to be very full of producing and directing. He was never going to be content just as an actor.

Laurence Olivier
1950, Notley Abbey

Polaroid shot of Larry outside Notley. He bought it while he was doing *Henry V*. Perfect house casting. We saw many dawns at Notley.

Mary, Peter Ustinov and Mary *1950*
Another Polaroid.

Hayley *1950, Woolacombe beach*
What a pose! The Little Mermaid.

Mary, Hayley, Jonathan and Nanny Workman *1950, Woolacombe*
In 1950 I bought a stereophonic camera. You used a special viewer to get the most marvellous 3D effect. This was one of the first shots taken with the camera above Woolacombe beach in the summer of 1950.

Juliet, Hayley and Jonathan *1950*

We moved from Cheyne Walk after only 18 months to The Wick on Richmond Hill, a staggeringly beautiful Georgian house built for the King's mistress. Lord Louis Grieg, the late King's ADC, was living in Richmond Park and told us The Wick was for sale.

The Wick *1950, Richmond*

This is the amazing view from The Wick on Richmond Hill looking over the River Thames. On a clear day we could see Windsor Castle.

Jonathan, Hayley and Pippa *1952*

Jonathan, Hayley and Pippa, Wyn's daughter. She was a sweet and beautiful little girl. Died tragically young a few years ago.

Me, Juliet, Hayley and Jonathan *1952*

Mary took this on the Thames. Jonathan is wearing the HMS Kelly hat given him by Lord Mountbatten.

Me, Mary, Larry, Vivien and (right) Noel
1952, Café de Paris

This was taken at Noel's first night in cabaret ... extraordinary response, the
room was continually on its feet.

**Me, Mary, Tamara Tonararo, Margaret Lockwood, Rock Hudson, Googie
Withers, John Maccallum, Vivien Leigh and Terence Morgan**
1953 The Empire London (left)

The fifties were a very glamorous time in the industry. There were premiers
weekly, parties at the Café Royal and Café de Paris.

Mary and Juliet at Richmond *1951*

Johnny carrying my polo sticks *1952*

Sussex House Farm *1953*

I was playing in a revival of *Charley's Aunt* when we bought a wonderful Elizabethan farm with 175 acres in Sussex. The children were ecstatic, especially Hayley and Johnny. I would drive home from Brighton after the show, then get up and go milking at 5am! I wanted to learn everything about farming. Over the years we increased the size of the farm to 500 acres.

Me *1950*

Me on Rosetta. I started playing polo at The Wick, much to the horror of various film production insurance companies. I actually went crazy about the sport and became really quite good, a 2 handicap.
Eventually I had to give it up after someone was killed in a match I was playing in and the press took a picture of me.

Tyrone Power, Linda Christian and Romina *1951*

I remember Ty Power as an incredibly generous man. One time I admired a watch he was wearing (a 'cocktail' it was called). He took the watch off his wrist and insisted I have it.

Lilli, Rex and Carey Harrison
1952, Switzerland and Portofino
Great stereo slides.

The Coronation 1953, London

I was appearing in *Damascus Blade* at the St James, a lousy play Larry Olivier produced. It did badly, ran no time at all, a complete dud... Anyway, It was a thrilling day, lots of people, an English day...a new Queen...Hayley remembers the sailors (naturally) in the parade, and that it was raining, making the white drip off their hats all over their uniforms. This was also where Noel's classic remark was made when asked who the little chap was riding in a carriage next to the enormous Queen of Tonga. 'That's her lunch,' he said.

Joan Greenwood 1953

The Uninvited Guest was the fourth play that Mary wrote. We assembled a marvellous cast, including the delectable Joan Greenwood, took it on the road, had a big success and came back to London where we were bashed by the critics. The character I played had been in prison for a long time, very white face, shadows under the eyes and a bright red wig. That was all part of the character. I well remember a review which read: ' While Mr. Olivier is away in Australia, there are some very strange things going on in his theatre. I think he should come back and have a look at it because it's a play by Mary Hayley Bell called *The Uninvited Guest*. Mr. Mills wanders about the stage looking like a bewildered carrot.' Mary and I were sitting up in bed at The Wick, and we both roared with laughter. We laughed all day. On Monday I went to the theatre, spirits high. The cast were in good cheer. In my dressing room, I started putting on the white make-up, adding shadows under my eyes, then I got to the wig stage, picked it up, put it on my head, looked in the mirror and broke into floods of tears. I just managed to pull myself together to go on stage but I was, for the next hour and a half, a bewildered carrot...

Me and Charles Laughton / 1954, 'Hobson's Choice'

Mary's best shot of me (*left*) in *Hobson's Choice*. As luck would have it, Robert Donat was ill and unable to play Willy Mossop. David Lean cabled me while I was in Portofino with Rex and Lilli. Within 48 hours I was in the make-up chair at Shepperton studios having a pudding-basin haircut.

It was the first time David and I had worked with Charles Laughton. I think David was slightly in awe of him. Charlie was inclined to be a little bit method in his acting. He had one big comedy scene before the wedding and he said to me, 'Johnnie, this is a very good scene isn't it? I see it as "stars and rockets, stars and rockets", don't you, David?' David looked blank and said, 'Yes…yes…stars and rockets.' He didn't have the slightest idea what Charlie was talking about. Neither did I! He was a fascinating actor to work with. Absolutely brilliant one minute and slightly amateur the next, but I've never seen anybody like him. You couldn't take your eyes off him.

Without doubt, this is one of the films I'm most proud of.

Me and Ralph Thomas *(right)*
With Jonathan *(left)*
1954, Above Us the Waves'
Above Us the Waves was the story of
the midget submarines during the
war. Those chaps had to be the
bravest of all, stuck in little tubes...

Me, Van Johnson and Deborah Kerr *'The End of the Affair', 1955*

This was the first time I worked with Van. We became good friends. After the
film was finished, we all went on holiday to the South of France. Van was
wearing red socks. He said he always wore them on stage, and from then on, I
did the same. When he was being shown around Larry's Notley Abbey he just
couldn't believe how old it all was - the 10th century tower etc. Anyway, he
spotted a haystack in a nearby field and said, ' My God, look at that old
haystack!' It was funny at the time…

Me and Major P.R.Reid, '*The Colditz Story***', 1955**

Major Reid, wrote the book, *The Colditz Story.* He was a senior British officer in the German prison and the one who planned the mass escape. I played him in the film. Guy Hamilton directed.

Me *1956, 'It's Great to Be Young'*

I was sent a script in 1956 for a musical called *It's Great to Be Young* to be shot at Elstree on a very, very small budget. I liked it but didn't think it had much of a chance, so I turned it down. They were very keen on having me, apparently, and my agent said he could get me a percentage of the picture if I did it. I said if I did it, I would take my straight salary. It was a gigantic financial success, and ran in Tokyo alone for two years. Had I taken my manager's advice I would now be a multi-millionaire.

Me and Bryan Forbes, '*The Colditz Story***', 1955**

In the 50s, a star carried a film. I'd had a few commercial flops and, at one point, I heard the phrase 'box office poison' linked to my name. When Ivan Foxwell offered me the part he said he could only pay me half of my usual salary. He was tough as nails. Anway, I swallowed my pride and accepted. The film was a big hit and I was back in favour again.

Jonathan *1955, St Moritz*

I always felt the light was special in three particular places – Switzerland, Australia and South Africa… Great still, although I say so myself!

Me, Mary, Juliet Hayley and Jonathan *1955, St Moritz*

This was the year I got my Kandahar (the silver medal awarded by the Ski Patrol). I skied with the British team and became pretty good. It was while I was skiing that I heard one of my daughter's had broken her leg. It was Hayley. Her screams were so bad when she was having her leg straightened by the Ski Rescue people that Juliet and Johnny never went skiing again during the entire holiday and learnt to ice skate instead.

Me and Henry Fonda *1956, 'War and Peace'*

In *War and Peace*, I had a small part with a big scene in prison with Henry Fonda. I was pretty
nervous. Everyone else had been working on the film for about six months. It went well, I thought,
and afterwards Fonda and I had lunch together, but Hank wasn't saying anything, dead quiet. I asked if
something was the matter, and he said he had had a problem with the scene we did together. Alarmed,
I asked what. He said I was the first person in six months to look him in the eye during a scene and it
had thrown him completely! Those were the days when quite a few actors even went as far as asking
you not to look them in the eye.

Juliet *1956, 'Alice Through the Looking Glass', Chelsea Palace*

Juliet was wonderful as Alice and had the priceless opportunity of working with some great musical comedy stars – Binnie Hale, Leslie Henson, Walter Chrisham, Michael Dennison as Humpty Dumpty and Dulcie Gray as the White Queen.

Me and Ronald Hines *1955, 'The Baby and the Battleship', Italy*

Curiously, Ronald Hines was my senior clerk at R.W.Paul in 1925. I was sent the script by Elstree studios. It was awful, but the idea was good. I gave the script to Bryan to do a rewrite with a character called 'Puncher'. The film was made in Naples, Italy, with Dickie, Bryan and Lionel Jeffries.

Haymaking *1957, Sussex House Farm*

What a wonderful summer we had at the farm. This was the first
slide (left) that Johnny found in the attic at Hills House.
Haymaking and harvest time was always the best time of the year…
long, warm days in one of the most beautiful parts of England and
a pint of bitter in the barn at the end of the day.

Me and Bernard Lee *1957, 'Dunkirk', Rye*

Bernard Lee was a very under-rated actor because he was a little too frequently on the juice. Mickey Balcon (Sir Michael) was the producer, and everyone was bowing and scraping. He was there all the time keeping a beady eye on everything.

One day I was about to shoot a fairly complicated scene, a long tracking shot talking to Bernie Lee and he wasn't anywhere to be found. They sent out five motorbikes to tour the area. Finally they discovered him in a pub, playing the piano, half smashed, and it was only 11 o'clock in the morning. They collared him, poured water over him, got him back on the beach. Balcon was there and Bernie said, 'Hello Sir Mick, how's it going?' Everyone was holding their breath. Bernie didn't have a clue what was going on. He asked what the dialogue was, and I had to write everything down for him with the cues on the back of a Players cigarette packet. He said, 'Give me a moment,' and went off behind a trailer. In two minutes he came back word perfect and gave a marvellous performance. That was Bernie Lee.

Shooting the beach scene *1957, 'Dunkirk', Rye*

Me and Troops, *1957 'Dunkirk', Rye*

This has to be one of Mary's best shots. Fabulous. That day we had 4000 troops working as extras. On cue we would all run up the beach and hit the deck when the mines started to go off. Hundreds of mines had been planted all over the beach to look like bombs being dropped by German dive-bombers. These 'special effects' mines were quite dangerous and we were told they had been marked with little red sticks about 5 inches high. 'Stay away at least 15 yards from the sticks when you fling yourselves down.' The whistle went and I found myself in the middle of thousands of men charging up the beach. On cue I hurled myself down, right on top of a mine! Somebody had trodden on the stick and, boom, up I went in the air. That is when my hearing started to go. I burst an eardrum at Dunkirk and didn't get decorated! It was a sensational shoot and you couldn't tell it wasn't the other side of the channel.

Mary, Hayley, Jonathen, Rex and Kay Kendall Harrison *1957, Portofino, Italy*

Rex had just married Kay Kendall and he invited us for a holiday to his villa in Portofino. He thought the family atmosphere would be good. We all drove down together and, when we got to the villa, Rex showed us around the house. Unfortunately, when he got to their bedroom he opened the lavish closet and Kay was showered with Lilli's underwear. Not a good start. Kay was furious. Anyway, later at dinner and after a tremendous amount of wine, we were talking about marriage and I said Mary and I had been married for nearly twenty years. Rex turned to me and said, 'That's very smug isn't?' Well from then on it went downhill and we ended up moving into a hotel in town, later that night. The next morning Rex came down to the hotel for breakfast and apologized.

We used to take Rex's speedboat on long trips along the coast, stopping for lunch in some marvellous spots.

Me *1957, 'Ice Cold in Alex',*
The Sahara Desert, Libya

Just a great shot (above) from Mary. It
took a week to shoot the ambulance
going up the hill. Incredible heat and
always knee-deep in sand.

We spent six weeks under canvas
which meant scorpions, 100 degree heat
in the day, 40 degrees at night and sand
everywhere, most places where you don't
want it...it was the best location ever.

Harry Andrews and Tony Quayle
1957, 'Ice Cold in Alex', The Sahara Desert, Libya

Me, Sylvia Syms And Harry Andrews
1957, 'Ice Cold in Alex', The Sahara Desert, Libya

J. Lee Thompson *1957, 'Ice Cold in Alex', The Sahara Desert, Libya*

Lee always had everything worked out in his head, a meticulous director. The minefield scene was brilliantly directed.

Me and Sylvia Sims *1957, 'Ice Cold in Alex', The Sahara Desert, Libya.*

This is the famous four-button shot which got censored. We had to re-shoot it at Elstree studios with only three buttons undone. How times have changed.

Mary, Harry Andrews and Anthony Quayle *1957, Leptis Magna, Libya*

Dorothy Hyson Quayle
1957, Leptis Magna, Libya
Tony Quayle's wife. Still ravishing.

Me *1957, Leptis Magna, Libya*

Great still from Mary of me at the Roman remains of Leptis Magna. We were the only people at these extraordinary ruins, treasures literally lying around on the ground. Wonderful place for photographs.

Me and Margaret Lockwood *(top)*
1958, 'Night of a Hundred Stars',
London Palladium (above)

A couple of swells.
   With Larry, and then (right)
with Larry again, Vivien Leigh and
Tyrone Power in the boater and
striped jacket.

Overleaf: **Me and Horst Buchholtz** *1958,*
'Tiger Bay', Cardiff

Hayley fell madly in love with Horst, who
gave a terrific performance in the film.

Hayley *1958, 'Tiger Bay', Cardiff*

I think even David Bailey wouldn't have
minded taking this one.

Me, Hayley and J. Lee Thompson
1958, 'Tiger Bay', Cardiff

This was the first day's shooting on *Tiger Bay*. Lee was marvellous with Hayley, who was completely relaxed about the whole thing and just hummed a lot. I asked Lee if it was bothering him and he said, 'No no no - just keep her humming and we'll be all right.'

Hayley and Jonathan
1958
Johnny photographing Hayley's Golden Bear Award for *Tiger Bay.*

Me, Mary, Hayley and Larry *1958*
This shot was taken after the premier of *Tiger Bay*. It was a thrilling night. Hayley was just twelve.

Me and Bryan Forbes *1958, 'I was Monty's Double', Gibraltar*

Great screenplay by Bryan Forbes who also had a part in the film. We did one scene where we had to swim out to an enemy dinghy, overturn it and strangle the Germans in the water. As we started to wade out Bryan looked at me and said, 'I forgot to tell you something, I can't swim.'

Me *1959, 'Summer of the Seventeenth Doll',
Artransa Studios*

After working for a month on my
Australian accent and a month of
shooting, MGM in Hollywood called
to tell the director, Leslie Norman, that
they couldn't understand a word I was
saying! We ignored them and carried
on.

Me and Ernest Borgnine *1959, 'Summer
of the Seventeenth Doll', Artransa Studios*

This was taken in Sydney Harbour.
Ernie Borgnine was great fun to work
with. Angela Lansbury was also in the
film. Wonderful actress

Seaplane *1959*

This is one of
the planes
Mary, Hayley
and Johnny
flew in to join
me in
Australia while
I was filming
Summer of the

Seventeenth Doll. It took them eight days, with
one thing after another going wrong. By the time
they got to Fiji the captain refused to take the
plane up anymore. When I met them at Sydney
airport they couldn't stand straight.

Hayley and Jonathan
1959, Bangkok

On our way back to England we flew via Singapore, Bangkok and Hong Kong. In Singapore I bought Johnny his first camera, a Kodak.

The Floating Gardens
1959, Bangkok

Hayley *1959, 'Pollyanna', California*

Hayley was terribly nervous and quite ghastly in her first scene with Karl Malden on *Pollyanna*. It wasn't easy suddenly being a star in Hollywood, in a big Disney movie, with a huge star like Malden. The director, David Swift, came to me, quite worried, and said, 'I can't get anywhere with Hayley. Is she all right? Is she very nervous?'

I talked to Hayley and said, ' What's the matter? You're like a great big cabbage, nothing's happening!' But after lunch there was a transformation. This shot *(left)* was her response to the cabbage line!

Hayley, Jane Wyman and Richard Egan *1959, 'Pollyanna', California (opposite)*

All the cast were absolutely wonderful to Hayley. I can remember one scene where the whole crew were crying after a take. Hayley couldn't figure it out. She won a Special Oscar in 1960 for her performance.

Hayley and Walt *1959, Disneyland*

One Sunday during the shooting of *Pollyanna*, Walt took Hayley, Jonathan, Mary and me to Disneyland. The best thing about it was we didn't have to wait in any queues. Everything was going smoothly until we got to the bumper cars. Walt took us through a side gate, past a line that went for miles, and over to an empty car. One of the attendants immediately rushed up and shouted, 'You can't jump the line! Who do you think you are, Walt Disney?!'

Mary *1959, Hollywood*

One of my all-time favourites of Mary in the pool at our house in Benedict Canyon, Beverly Hills.

Mary and Jimmy Granger *1959, Hollywood*

Mary and Jimmy at Niven's.

Fondest love

David Niven *1959, Hollywood*

Funnily enough what I remember most about Niven's house in Beverly Hills was the pool's changing room. On the men's side he had this see-through mirror. We spent quite a bit of time in there, depending on the female guests of the day of course.

Niven was a great practical joker, and I was quite famous for lighting farts. The preparation is funny on its own. You have to lie on your back with your legs in the air trying to light the thing. This one time at David's when I clicked the lighter, the flame I ignited was like a Bunsen burner – a foot long and blue. Sensational. Niven laughed so much he had to be taken to hospital.

One time I was stuck at the top of the Jungfrau during *Scott* and the weather closed in on us for four days. The boys were getting bored and fed up, no radios, nothing and I said, 'Look, I'll do my trick.' It was a bit of luck because I'd had some grapes for lunch and they worked a treat. I did a terrific one and it put the whole unit right.

David Niven *1959, Hollywood (left)*

Niven in flight. What more is there to say? David gave this to me. A classic. I was there the day the picture was taken by one of the Hollywood press. He couldn't get rid of them so David said he would give them one more shot and then they would have to leave. Typical Niven, he always knew how to deliver the goods.

The Treehouse *1959, 'Swiss Family Robinson', Tobago*

The enormous tree house was so brilliant it was recreated in Disneyland and is still one of the attractions there. Sometimes Johnny and Kevin Corcoran used to sleep in it at night.

Me *1959, 'Swiss Family Robinson', Tobago*

A month after Hayley started *Pollyanna* in Hollywood, I was offered the part of the father in Disney's '*Swiss Family Robinson*', set in the West Indies on Tobago. Unspoiled paradise. We rented a house on the beach on the south side of the island. The filming took so long that both Johnny and Hayley (below) ended up going to the local school where they were the only white children.

THE 1960s

Me, Hayley and Hywel Bennett *1967, 'The Family Way'*

Hywel was very good as Hayley's fiancé in the film

Me and Dirk Bogarde
1960, 'The Singer not the Song' Spain

We shot the film in a beautiful Spanish village. The villagers really believed I was a priest, and I hated to disabuse them. Marlon Brando was going to play the other lead and I was thrilled because he was one of my favorite actors. Unfortunately he walked away, and Dirk Bogarde replaced him at the last minute. He of course was rather miscast as the tough, leather-clad baddie.

Me, Mary, Hayley, Jonathan, Lord Fraser, Sir Frederick Wells, Sheila Attenborough, Zelia Raye, Roma Beaumont, Louise Browne, and Tyrone Guthrie *1960 'This is Your Life'*

In 1960 I was caught for *This is Your Life* and it was brilliantly done. I had been around filming at Pinewood studios. We finished at 6.30 and my driver, Jolly, came into the dressing room and said, 'I'm terribly sorry. We're being delayed by at least three-quarters of an hour because of a puncture on the Rolls.' When we left, finally, I was not in the best of moods. It had been a long day, and I wanted to get home. At the studio gate we stopped. There was a blaze of light and about five cameras, and then Eamon Andrews stepped forward and said, 'John Mills – This is Your Life.'

Me and Alec Guinness *1960 'Tunes of Glory'*

Both Alec and I had marvellous parts and the film was a big success. It was the year of the Venice Film Festival and the word was going round that Alec would win best actor.

Alec hated publicity. 'We'll just fly over to Venice quietly, the two of us,' Ronnie Neame (the director) said, 'very low key, get a nice hotel and you just go and pick up the award.' After a lot of persuasion, Alec agreed. As they taxied into the airport there was a whole crowd of people out there and a brass band. 'What's that?' Alec asked. 'I don't know,' Ronnie replied. 'They must have a VIP arriving or something like that.' When Alec descended the steps of the plane, the mob rushed him. He had to march right across the aerodrome in front of the band. He was white with fury! 'It was nothing to do with me, Alec,' Ronnie claimed, 'but that's it for the trip.' That evening off they went to the cinema, sitting right in the front row, and the presenter come on and said, '*Tunes of Glory* is a very important English picture, and we're happy to announce that the winner of the Best Actor award is - John Mills.' Poor old Alec had to go up and make a gracious acceptance speech and pick up an enormous silver cup for me.

Me and Larry *1961, France*

Mary had a nasty habit of sneaking up on people and she caught us here on the balcony of the Cap Estelle Hotel in the South of France. It was Larry's first holiday abroad with new wife, Joan Plowright. We spent the most hilarious, drunken week at a most marvellous hotel. Without a doubt Larry was one of the funniest people I ever knew, and, frankly, I've met a lot of funny people.

Top: **Mary, Larry and Joan Plowright** *1961, Cap Ferrat*

Above: **Mary, Hayley, David Niven and Joan Plowright** *1961, Cap Ferrat*

Niven had a beautiful house on the sea with his own harbour.

Left: **Me, Larry and Joan** *1961 Cap Ferrat*

Endless Blanc de Blanc.

Me and Abuabutayai
1961, 'Ross', Eugene O'Neill Theatre, New York (above)

Me *1961, 'Ross', Eugene O'Neill Theatre, New York (left)*

I nearly turned *Ross* down. I hadn't been on the stage in eight years and the idea of opening cold on Broadway, without a warm-up tour, was terrifying. David Merrick, the producer, thought the show was too expensive to take on the road. It was while we were on holiday with Larry and Joan that Larry persuaded me to do it. 'You'll never do another thing on the stage if you don't do this,' he said. And he was right.

James Mason *1961, 'Tiara Tahiti', Tahiti (opposite)*

The first and only time I worked with James Mason was on *Tiara Tahiti*. I think he was a very shy and complex man with enormous charm. And, of course, one of the best film actors ever.

I remember one evening we were at a dinner together, given by Ivan Foxwell, on the beach. Very romantic setting. After a dinner I sang a song I'd written, accompanying myself on the ukelele. When I finished, I was surprised to see Jimmy had tears rolling down his cheeks. For all his success, I think he had quite a difficult life.

Me *1961, 'Tiara Tahiti', Tahiti*
South Pacific paradise, but not as nice as
Tobago.

Rosenda Monteros *1961, 'Tiara Tahiti',
Tahiti*

Rosenda Monteros was cast as the girl in
the film, couldn't speak a word of
English, but looked very good indeed as
a Tahitian.

Me and Mary *1961, 'Tiara Tahiti', Tahiti*
One of my favourite shots of Mary and me, taken by Johnny in front of our thatched beach hut.

Hayley and Jonathan
1962, Beverly Hills

This is one of those lucky shots where everything, including the dive, turns out perfectly.

Mary, Jonathan, Hayley and Me *1962, Beverly Hills*

There are some days that live vividly in one's memory. This day at Gladys Cooper's house is one of them. We all did funny poses for this sequence of shots in Gladys's wonderful garden overlooking the golf course.

Hayley and Mary 1962, 'Summer Magic', Disney Studios (above)

Hayley and Walt Disney 1962, 'Summer Magic', Disney Studios (left)
Hayley on her way to work during *Summer Magic*.

Me *1962, 'The Valiant', Italy*

The only time I played a captain was in this not very good film. Enjoyed working with Bob Shaw. What an actor, full of power and character. Not a nice location but Johnny took a couple of wonderful shots.

Rex Harrison and Rachel Roberts *1962 The Farm, Sussex*

Rex came down to the farm to help christen the pool with his wife, Rachel Roberts. The lunch went on and on, and ON.

Mary, Juliet, Hayley and Jonathan *1962, The Farm, Sussex*

Larry Olivier and David Niven
1963, France

I took these at Niven's harbour in front
of his house in the South of France. It
was during this holiday that Prince
Rainier and Grace Kelly came over one
evening for drinks. When they arrived,
Larry was just getting out of the water
without his swimming trunks. They'd
come off in the bay somewhere.
Rainier and the Princess were standing
right in front of him as Larry emerged
from the sea and bowed gracefully.
Perhaps his best entrance ever!

Jack Hawkins
1963, Rome

I first met Jack Hawkins at Billy's Café in London. It was 1929, and I was about to go to India with the Quaints. Jack was rehearsing *Young Woodley*, directed by the infamous Basil Dean. Dean was a terror. After the end of the first act on the opening night he collected the cast together and said, 'Listen, I want to tell you something. You are all a bunch of amateurs, the audience is half asleep, there is nothing happening at all! It's a disaster, the bloody play will be off by tomorrow!' Naturally the second act was electric and the curtain came down on the hit of the season. Jack and Dee Hawkins became very close friends of ours.

Me, Tom Courtenay and Patrick Moore *1964, 'King Rat', Hollywood*

Me, Gerald Simms and Patrick Moore *1964, 'King Rat', Hollywood*

In the film, one of the officers is very much disliked by the rest of the inmates and we were told they had found a baby rabbit and they had cooked it specially for us and it would be delicious. We were thoroughly enjoying it when somebody dropped the word in that we *were* actually eating rats. Bryan was very upset and dashed out and bought a Magnum of champagne, which we swilled back very fast because I think we really were eating rats!

Tom Courtenay and James Fox *1964, 'King Rat', Hollywood*

King Rat showed how unpredictable this funny old business can be. It was a wonderful script, a great cast and one of the best directorial jobs Bryan Forbes has ever done. It was shot on location in California, where the studio constructed a replica of Changi jail. One morning we went out and discovered that everything was turning brown when it was supposed to be lush jungle. It was worse the next day so they hired helicopters and sprayed everything with green paint, which made shooting a bit sticky. Everybody loved the picture but it wasn't a success. The only thing I can put it down to is that there was no gorgeous, glamorous girl, no love interest.

Me and Dickie Attenborough
1964, Cap D'Ail, France

This is a very unusual picture of my greatest friend, Dickie, during one of his rare holiday outings.

Doreen Hawkins *1964, Cap D'Ail, France*

Doreen has been a great friend for many years, the wife of Jack Hawkins. They owned a villa near the Nivens.

The villa *1964, Cap D'Ail, France (left)*

In 1964 Hayley bought a lovely villa in Cap D'Ail near Monte Carlo.

Bryan Forbes and The Kids *1964, 'Whistle Down the Wind', Clitheroe, Lancashire*

This was Bryan's first picture as a director. Dickie suggested him, I knew Bryan well and I agreed it was a good idea. He was a marvellous photographer and Dickie felt that he would be able to handle the children well, which he did.

Hayley and Alan Bates *1964, 'Whistle Down the Wind', Clitheroe, Lancashire*

Hayley by this time had made several films. She felt she was too big and too old for the part and wouldn't fit in well with the other children, which of course was ridiculous, She turned in a remarkably fine performance. By this time she knew what acting was all about but still retained that marvellous simplicity she always projected on the screen.

Alan was a vastly experienced actor in the theatre and he took to filming like a duck takes to water. I remember thinking at the time, this man can't go wrong. Bryan Forbes will tell you that all you had to do with Alan was point him towards the set.

Hayley, our Nan and Charlie *1964, 'Whistle Down the Wind', Clitheroe, Lancashire*

I can't say enough how much *Whistle Down the Wind* means to our family. First the wonderful book, then Hayley in the film directed by Bryan Forbes and produced by Dickie Attenborough, a big success; and now, all these years later, Andrew Lloyd Webber's thrilling musical. What a wonderful journey Mary's story has had.

Hayley, Lionel Jeffries and Harry Andrews
1964, 'The Truth About Spring', Greece

Opposite: **Me, Lionel and Harry**
1964, 'The Truth About Spring', Greece

Lionel was a brilliant actor who could play a variety of roles from low comedy to high drama. His timing was superb. Harry was wonderful too as the other bad guy.

One day it was terribly rough and we hadn't got a shot in the can all morning. Everybody was feeling queasy. The chef arrived at lunch time with a huge pot of paella, which he set up on deck and was immediately sick into it.

Children *1965, 'Sky West and Croocked' Badminton*

Me and Ralph Richardson
1964, 'The Wrong Box', Bath

Ralph was, as everybody knows, the last of the great eccentrics. In one hilarious scene, I had to garrotte, poison and stab him. I remember feeling rather embarrassed that I was having to do these terrible things to the great man with whom I had never before acted in my life.

But he didn't hold it against me, and later Mary and I were invited to dinner at his lovely house in Hampstead. After several large gins before dinner, we got stuck into Ralph's favourite claret. I can't think how many glasses we emptied. Then he said, 'You play the piano, dear boy, don't you? Let's go into the music room. I'm a performer on the violin.' There was a nice piano in one corner and a big screen in the other. Ralph disappeared behind the screen and shouted, 'Right, I'm ready.' 'OK, Ralphie,' I replied. 'What shall we play?' And he said, 'Oh...just play, just play and I'll follow.' So I played 'Auld Lang Syne' and from the other side of the screen came 'Dinah'. He played happily to the end and we gave a recital for an hour, playing quite different things. All I saw of Ralph was clouds of 965 Dunhill wafting over the top of the screen. He claimed afterwards to have had the best evening of his life.

Me, Michael Caine, Nanette Newman, Peter Cook, Dudley Moore and Tony Hancock *1964, 'The Wrong Box', Bath (opposite)*

Bryan assembled a really great cast.

147

Me, Hayley and Ian McShane
1965, 'Sky West and Crooked', Badminton

Sky West and Crooked I made while under contract to Rank. I have always believed in my career that you should never go on the floor without a totally tight script and, in this case, I was unable to do that. I was under contract, they had a gap in the schedule and I was persuaded against my better judgement to start filming eight weeks before I was ready. And inevitably it showed in the finished picture. I had Hayley's career in my hands and my wife's story. It wasn't a very bad film but it could have been a great deal better. Having said all that, Hayley turned in a fine performance and Ian McShane made an excellent debut as a gypsy.

Me *1967, 'The Family Way', Bolton*

The Boulting brothers, the 'terrible twins', approached me first for this picture, which was very good for my morale at that time. They also said they would like Hayley. I remember my agent, Laurence Evans, going to see them to negotiate on my behalf. When I asked him how it had gone, he said, 'Fine, it was like being interviewed by two headmasters.' Roy was a sensitive director, and on the ball and very, very helpful. Whatever performance I gave he had a great deal to do with.

Hayley, Roy and John Boulting *1967*

This is a still of Hayley with the Boulting brothers, at this time the owners of British Lion films. Hayley married Roy in 1971.

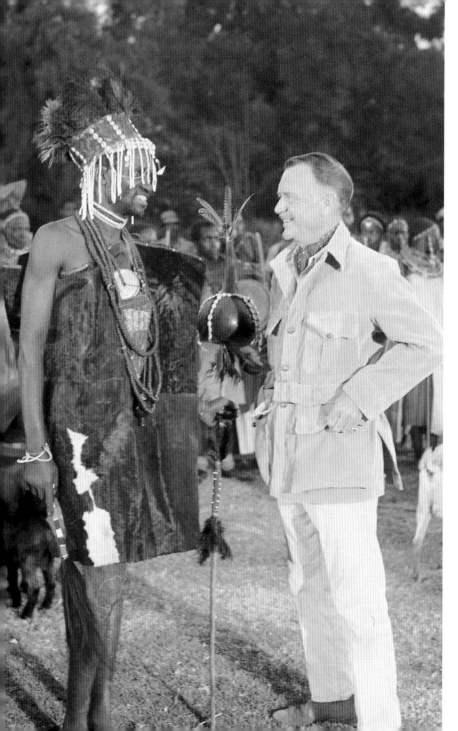

Me and a Masai Chief *1967, 'Africa, Texas Style!', Kenya*

Cowboy in Africa was what I used to call one of my 'tax films'. The top rate then was something like 87% or 88%. Ridiculous. Laurence Evans said to me, 'I've got another film for you, but I wouldn't do it this year, if I were you, because, honestly Johnny, you won't get a penny out of it.' But if I said no, about 200 people would be out of a job, and I had never been to Kenya. Hayley came out too, all expenses paid by the production company, if she agreed to be in a couple of shots, which she did. They gave us a plane when we had finished shooting to go wherever we wanted. We flew to the Teva River, hunting with cameras. The real white hunters built big fires at night to keep the animals at bay. There were lions all around. I remember Mary walking up the dry bed of the Teva River with huge dry elephant turds in her arms, which she reckoned, would help keep the fire going. She became known as the 'Turd woman of the Teva' from then on.

Masai extras *1967, 'Africa, Texas Style!', Kenya*

The Masai
1967, 'Africa, Texas Style!', Kenya

Elephant
1967, 'Africa, Texas Style!', Kenya

Me *1967, 'Africa, Texas Style!', Kenya*

I bought a new Leica before going to Kenya and shot everything and everyone in sight, mostly in black and white.

Sir Peter and Lady Daubeney and Noel Coward, *1968*

Peter joined the 201st Coldstream Guards at 18 and as a Lieutenant went out to Italy. In the battle for Salerno (Battipaglia) he was severely wounded, losing an arm. Barely alive, he was taken to a military hospital, where, a week later he heard that Noel Coward was entertaining the troops about three miles away. Peter walked the three miles, fainting two or three times en-route but ended up seeing the great Noel Coward. The following week, Noel visited the hospital and was introduced to the young Peter Daubeney who was back in bed. He was very moved and discovered that Peter, who had been an actor before the war, was keen on getting into the theatre and becoming a producer. When he got back to England, Noel was very helpful and Peter went on to become a very successful producer indeed and with his lovely wife, Molly, they started the World Theatre Season, bringing plays from every country in the world to London. It was a colossal success and he was rightly knighted not long after that.

Mia Farrow *1968*

At the time Mia was married to Frank Sinatra or was it André Previn. Anyway she was having a few ups and downs.

Tommy Steele *1968, Hollywood*

Tommy Steele bought a house in Richmond when we were at The Wick. We met up in Hollywood one night and found ourselves talking about music, and I asked him if he played the guitar? He paused for a moment, then said, 'Well I used to…'.

Me, Dickie and Thorley Waters *1968, 'Oh! What a Lovely War', Brighton*

Me *1968, 'Oh! What a Lovely War', Brighton*

I played Field Marshal Haig in Dickie Attenborough's brilliant film of the play.

Now if I was asked to name a highlight of 'Still Memories' I would probably say *Oh! What a Lovely War* because it is a highlight in every kind of way. Mary and I went to the theatre to see a performance of *Oh! What a Lovely War* put on by the brilliant Joan Littlewood.

Afterwards, the three of us had supper together and decided it would make a marvellous film. It was a very daring proposition, but we went ahead with it anyway, obtained the rights and talked to a marvellous writer whom we knew very well, called Len Deighton. He liked the idea enormously and we worked on the script together for about six months. Then I had to rush off to Hollywood because I had a tax problem and I had to earn a lot of money rather quickly. Dickie Attenborough was dying to direct a picture and I sent him the nearly finished script.

He lived at the bottom of the hill on Richmond Green and we were at 'The Wick' at the top end. I sent it to him on the Saturday night and on Sunday morning at 8 o'clock, the phone rang and Dickie said, 'I've got to do it.' I had to take off for Hollywood but Dickie said, 'You must get back soon because you have to play Haig.' Every week he called up to say, 'It's going well but when are you coming home?' He'd managed to get Larry on board, and the moment Olivier agreed, every actor in England and every actress of note said yes. So he assembled the most fantastic cast – Sir Ralph Richardson, Sir John Gielgud, Sir John Clements, Kenny More, Jack Hawkins, and all the dames you can think of. I did get back eventually and they stuck an enormous nose on me and a big white moustache and I played Field Marshall Haig.

Me and Larry Olivier *1968, 'Oh! What a Lovely War', Brighton*

On the back of a print of this picture Larry wrote. ' From the look on my face, you might think I was propositioning you, from the look on yours, there can be no doubt about it!'

155

Dearest Knob,
You have been
at it again!

And many more
please!
This one –
"Ryans
Daughter"
love,
David
1969.

Me and David Lean *1969, 'Ryan's Daughter', Ireland*

I got the part because of Mary. We were in Rome and making a dreadful picture, partly Italian. I couldn't understand a word anyone was saying, although it was supposed to be in English. Mary heard that David Lean was in Rome so she rang him up. He said come over and have dinner. Robert Bolt was there too. Mary said, 'What are you doing here David?' He said he was writing a script with Robert. 'Anything in there for Johnnie?' Mary asked. 'No.' he said, 'Now listen, David,' Mary said. 'I want to tell you something. Johnnie has made your career for you. He made four pictures which were all smash hits, then you pissed off to America and did some B pictures like *Bridge over the River Kwai*, *Zhivago* and other trash. Now what about Johnnie?' David thought and then said, 'No, there's nothing for him, honestly. I'd love to work with Johnnie again, but there isn't a part for him.' Mary said, 'Oh well, never mind, I tried.' David went very quiet then over coffee said, 'Knob, do you think you could play a village idiot?' I replied, 'David, that's type casting!' And that is how it happened. Of course, MGM didn't want me. They didn't think I'd be right, they wanted a really grotesque, horrible-looking creature. So David said, 'Go and get yourself made up.' And I had a camera test. I had two heads, four noses and five eyes and MGM said, 'Right that's fine.'

Me, Sarah Miles and Trevor Howard *1969, 'Ryan's Daughter', Ireland*

Sarah loved Bob Mitchum and wasn't very keen on Christopher Jones, which of course was the opposite of what it should have been in the film. Trevor was concentrating on the juice a bit too much until he fell off his horse and broke his collar bone. That was the weekend Bob disappeared on a helicopter to Dublin for three days without telling anyone. It was an epic all right.

THE 1970s

Collecting the Oscar, On Tour with John Gielgud, Television Work, Good Companions, The Knighthood, Move to Hills House

Me *1977, 'The Devil's Advocate', Italy*

Me and Oscar, *1970, Hollywood*

Best supporting actor for *Ryan's Daughter.* My bandaged finger is because a hotel doorman slammed it in the taxi door.

Me and Dick Cavett *1970, New York*

After *Ryan's Daughter* was released I was asked to go to New York to do some promotion. At that time Dick Cavett was the big talk show chap. David Lean went on first while I waited in the wings. Now David wasn't at his best on this kind of thing, he became very technical, and I could see Cavett getting quite anxious. Suddenly he said, 'David, we'll change the subject just for a moment, Let's talk about actors. Is there one in particular who you've worked with several times that you admire?' I'm there waiting with one foot raised and David says, 'Yes, there is. Katherine Hepburn.' It came as a bit of a shock to me but Cavett was completely thrown. I pranced on anway, bowed, thanked David for the nice introduction and then went totally mad. 'Do you have a piano on the stage?' I said. 'Yes,' Cavett replied. So I said, 'Do you mind if I go and play something?' He said, 'No, I'd be delighted.' I sang the song I did in *The Baby and the Battleship*, a lullaby which became a family favourite. It brought the house down.

Juliet *1972, 'Avanti', Italy*

Another film that should have been a big success, it was a marvellous opportunity for Juliet to work with the great Jack Lemmon and Billy Wilder.

Juliet, Jack Lemmon, Billy Wilder and Clive Revill *1972, 'Avanti', Italy*

The only time I worked with Billy Wilder was on a TV film of Somerset Maugham's *The Letter*. Paul Scofield was set to be in it but, at the last minute he dropped out. CBS suggested Michael Rennie take his place. Rennie was a star who had never heard the word 'act'! He really was hopeless, so Billy found himself lumbered with this man and he said to me, 'Johnnie, what am I going to do?' Billy was in a panic, and decided to play Michael Rennie's part with me, so Michael could watch how it was done. After a week of this, it was supposed to be done live.

My nerves were in shreds and I had a sort of nervous breakdown. Mary took me to a specialist saying, 'My husband is falling apart at the seams.' He said, 'I'll give him an injection.' (He knew I was doing live TV with Billy Wilder.) He gave me a terrific shot and told me to lie down in the dark for a couple of hours, saying I would be all right. I was about to commit suicide, so I did what he told me and when I got up I was very calm, no more shakes. My first scene was with Siobhan McKenna. She had to come in and and say, 'You swine, you swine, I'm going to kill you. You've destroyed me, destroyed my life!' Then she picked up a gun and it went click. This was live TV, remember. She said, 'I don't know, you don't deserve to live,' and reached for a paper knife. At that moment the prop man, offstage, fired a gun, and I wasn't even on yet! But that doctor made sure I didn't mind at all.

I finally appeared in a bemused state for the scene with Michael Rennie, which I had played for many weeks with Billy. Now, when directing a television drama you have to leave it to the technical director for the last 24 hours. The producers said to Billy, 'You go into the box now, Mr. Wilder, and watch all the screens and then this brilliant TV tech director will take over. Billy said OK and this guy starts plotting the camera positions. After about 12 hours, Billy didn't like the positions at all. He said, 'No, no I don't like that.' This guy said, 'But Mr. Wilder, we only have another 10 hours before we go live.' Billy refused point blank. He got what he wanted. Ten hours later we went live and in the middle of the play two cameras collided head on at about 20 mph.

Me and John Gielgud *1972, 'Veterans', The Royal Court (left)*

I had worked with Sir John very little and I had been an enormous admirer of his for years when I was suddenly offered this play, by Charles Wood. The Royal Court Theatre was a private theatre in which you could use any language you cared to use. In the commercial theatre at the time you couldn't even say, 'Jesus,' you had to say, 'Jeez.' 'Damn' was about the worst expletive. Gielgud and I had one scene, in which the f word occurred several times. He and I had rehearsed for three weeks, when the management came along and said, 'Boys, I'm afraid I have some bad news for you… you're not going to do this. Gielgud especially has a very long part and he's really not with it and, with a comedy, you have to be absolutely on your toes. I think we should go out on the road for three or four weeks.' We were appalled.

In Edinburgh we played for one hour and forty minutes to dead silence. The Scots didn't laugh at all. Next we went to the Opera House in Manchester. There the story was slightly different. The audience was restless, uneasy and there was a nasty feeling in the house. The curtain came down to little or no applause. I found a note in my dressing room saying, 'Dear Mr. Mills, you must be very hard up, I enclose a pound.' The next stop was Brighton. The management said,' Now listen, boys, you're having a very a rough time but when you get the Royal Opera House, you'll be at home. It's rather like the West End, they're rather sophisticated in Brighton. Have no fear, you'll have a good time.'

The first scene went splendidly. No problem, no bad language. For the next scene, on came Bob Hoskins, a young, unknown and he started, 'Put that f-ing chair over there and put that f-ing piano further over to the right and put that f-ing table over there…' There was a very rude noise from the front and people started muttering, and a large man in the front row of the circle got up all of a sudden and said, 'I tell you something, I'm going. This is absolutely terrible. Disgraceful language. To think I paid good money to see those two fuckers!'

Me, Mary and Bernard Miles *1972*
I worked with Bernard on *Run Wild Run Free*.

Me, George C. Scott and Faye Dunaway *1972, 'Oklahoma Crude', California*

Oklahoma Crude was one of those pictures where I never understood what happened. I thought it was a wonderful script, Stanley Kramer, a top director, thought it was, George C. Scott thought it was, Faye Dunaway did too. It was a disaster.

Me and Lilli Palmer
1972, 'The Zoo Gang', France

I played this filthy old French tramp who was trying to get into the Hotel de Paris in Nice. I looked dreadful with my teeth blacked out and a dreadful wig. They said, 'Action,' and I walked up the steps, but there were two doormen who hadn't been tipped off. They grabbed me and threw me out on my arse.

Me, Morecambe and Wise *1972*

Two of the funniest people in the business bar none. We did a take-off on *The Colditz Story*, Hysterical. Eric ad-libbed the whole time.

Me *1974, 'Good Companions', Her Majesty's Theatre, London*

The nine months I spent at Her Majesty's Theatre in the musical, *Good Companions* were undoubtedly the happiest eight months I have spent in the theatre. It was largely to do with a wonderful little lady called Judi Dench, who is not only a superb actress but also more fun than you can say. She is a great practical joker. I remember one scene in the first act where they all did a big number round and round the stage and I had a huge suitcase, which I had to pick up and drag on top of a truck, then half-conduct the number. The great moment came, they all started doing their routine and I went to pick up the suitcase and I couldn't shift it. It was full of bricks. I had the hell of a job getting it up on to the truck. Nobody left the theatre between the matinee and evening show because there were always tea parties in Judi's dressing room or mine. She was an absolute joy to be with.

Me, Mary, Juliet and Hayley *1976, London*

This is a still from the day I received my knighthood. I went to Buckingham Palace with Mary, Hayley and Juliet. Johnny was in America. It was a very hot day. I felt terribly nervous because I knew there were twelve of us being knighted and I was the only actor. I thought, 'I know I am going to screw this one up.' It was pure stage fright.

We were ushered into a small room where the Lord Chancellor was issuing the instructions on how to behave, what to do, the whole routine. I listened avidly as near the front as I could get. The Lord Chancellor had a very quiet voice and I was a bit deaf so I was just about to say, 'Sir, I'm afraid I didn't get that, would you mind repeating it…' when there was this crash on my shoulder. I turned round and there was Sir Douglas Bader DSO, DFC, two tin legs, one of the great heroes of the war and also a great friend of mine. He said, 'I was in the bathroom a few weeks ago and the phone rang and someone said, "Is that Sir Douglas? It's rather a delicate question." I said, "Fire away." So they said, "It's a question of the height of the stool. Can you manage it, it's about two feet high." So I said, "Wait a minute…" and left the phone dangling, came back about two minutes later and said, "Is that Buck House? I'm afraid it's no good, I've just fallen on my arse!"'

Douglas was on before me. He walked on with two sticks and he couldn't kneel down, so the Queen raised the sword on high and brought it down on each shoulder. It was very, very moving. I shall never forget it. I was on next and managed it all right, and the band played 'Why was he born so beautiful, Why was he born at all?'

Hills House, Denham Village
1976, Buckinghamshire

Hills House, Denham Village *1976, Buckinghamshire*

By 1976, Mary and I had really behaved like touring actors. We had lived in about fourteen or fifteen houses and at that particular time we were in a flat in Green Street which we detested because we hated London. We weren't going through a very happy time in terms of living conditions. Mary went to the dentist one day and she saw a copy of 'Country Life', on the front of which was a very, very beautiful house. 'My God,' she thought, 'that's Hills House in Denham Village, the house that Hayley was christened from.' She brought the magazine home to me and I said, 'That's it, that's it.'

We went down to see the place in February. There were nearly four acres covered in snow. Halfway across the orchard we stopped and I said to Mary, 'We can't afford this. It's divine but it 's too much.' I bought it the next day! We've been here for twenty-six years and it has been the most wonderful home to bring the grandchildren up in. Dickie Attenborough wrote in the visitor's book, 'Now this is it Johnnie. For God's sake don't move again.'

Hamlet and Mr.Chips
1976, Hills House, Buckinghamshire

Mary wrote two books about Hamlet, *Far Morning* and *Mr. Chips You and Me*.

Above: **Me and Barbra Streisand**

Frank and Barbara Sinatra *1977*

Frank sent me this still after he married Barbara Marx. Mary and I were staying in Noel's house during a hiatus while I was making an American TV pilot called *Dundee and The Culhane*. It didn't catch on. The phone rang one day and it was Frank. He said. 'Johnnie, have you heard anything from CBS?' I said, 'No,' and he replied, 'Well I have and I think you should know about it. They have cancelled the series, didn't they let you know?' I said, 'No.' He said, 'That's that son of a bitch. OK, Johnnie, I'll take care of him.' I said, 'No, I'm very happy. I don't want to go back to Hollywood.' He said, 'Never mind about that. He's a shithead and it is about time somebody took care of that guy.' It took me ten minutes to persuade him to lay off. This was Frank Sinatra. If he was a friend of yours he'd want to take care of you.

Me, Kenneth More and Michael Hordern *1977, Buckinghamshire*

Me and Larry *1978, London*

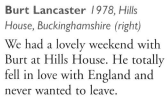

Me, Dulcie Gray and Michael Dennison *1978*

At the End of the Day was a comedy by William Douglas-Home, a story about two Prime Ministers - one who is leaving office and one who is entering. It was a great part for me as Harold Wilson and a great part for Dulcie Gray as Mary Wilson and a good part, but a small part for Michael Dennison playing Ted Heath.

Burt Lancaster *1978, Hills House, Buckinghamshire (right)*

We had a lovely weekend with Burt at Hills House. He totally fell in love with England and never wanted to leave.

Me, James Stewart, Judy Stewart and James Caan *1979*

Me, Mary, Harry Secombe, Lionel Jeffries, Robert Morley, Dickie Attenborough, Dickie Henderson, Flora Robson and Moira Lister *1979*

THE 1980s

Murder with Mirrors, Little Lies, Pygmalion in New York, The Polaroid Guest Books, Our Grandchildren

Me *1983 'Little Lies' Wyndam's Theatre*
Getting ready for a performance

David and Sandy Lean *1980, Bora Bora*

Mary and I had been filming in Australia and stopped off at a small paradise called Bora Bora, a tiny island near Tahiti. At the hotel we walked slap into David Lean. Neither of us could believe it. David was there with Robert Bolt writing the script of *Mutiny on the Bounty* which they never got to make.

Dougie and Mary Lee Fairbanks *1980, London*

Dougie and Mary Lee were living at No. 7 The Boltons which became the Mecca for society. The Queen dined there several times and it was very informal. One evening I remember Princess Margaret singing and playing the piano.

Me and Princess Margaret *1980, London*

Juliet and Maxwell *1980, Santa Barbara*

Juliet and Maxwell were married on a cliff overlooking the Pacific Ocean near Santa Barbara. Unfortunately I was working at the time. Johnny took this tremendous shot.

R.J. Wagner and Stefanie Powers *1981,*

I first met R.J. and Stefanie in Hollywood while they were doing their hit series. They were great friends of Juliet.

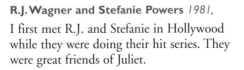

Mary and Pete Townshend *1982*

This is a picture of Mary and Pete Townshend, of The Who. We met at Elton John's birthday party. Pete became a great fan of Mary's in one evening and we saw quite a bit of him afterwards. In fact he bought The Wick on Richmond Hill.

I remember talking to John Reid, Elton's manager, and we asked him what he gave Elton for his birthday. He said, 'A new Ferrari' I said, 'My God, what a wonderful present. Where is it?' He said, 'On the lawn.' So we went outside and there was this Ferrari done up in a pink ribbon.

Me, Mary and Frank Sinatra *1980*

Mary and I were travelling back by train across America and, in the middle of the desert, the train broke down, about 2 in the afternoon, 118 in the shade, the air conditioning conked out.

I was in a carriage with Frank Sinatra and Walter Winchell, the columnist. Frank produced a bottle of Jack Daniels which we drank all night long waiting for the train to be fixed. We never looked back.

Me *1981, 'Gandhi', India*

It took Dickie Attenborough nearly 23 years to get the money to make *Gandhi*. He was the only person in the world who believed in it. Bryan Forbes was offered the script and turned it down. One Hollywood studio said to him, 'Dickie, what are you doing? Why do you want to make a picture about a failure in a night-shirt?' It collected about eight Oscars.

Me, Mary, James Mason and Clarissa Kaye *1982*

Me and Danny Kaye *1983*

Danny Kaye was a great friend and a friend of Larry and Vivien Olivier and we spent a lot of time together. We did several shows together at the London Palladium called *Night of a Hundred Stars*.

But Danny's great thing was that he could very easily have been one of the top chefs of the world. In fact he had a medallion saying he was a top chef and his house in Hollywood had the greatest kitchen I had ever seen in my life. He would invite friends to dinner and give them Chinese, French, Italian, whatever. It was a side of Danny that people didn't know; he was a fantastic cook.

Me and The Queen Mother *1984, London*

I was asked to give a speech at the Queen Mother's 90th birthday in Horseguards Parade. It needed to be very loving and familiar but never overstepping the mark. Not easy. When the time came, the ADC said, 'There'll be a BBC truck there and you just do it into the microphone.' Five minutes later I suddenly heard, 'Microphone Party!.....Shun!' and two great guardsmen came along and picked up the microphone. 'Right Turn!.....Forward March!' The penny started to drop. I was going to be there right in the middle of the parade ground. The band started up. My Achilles tendon had gone, but I managed to limp to time to my spot, twenty-five yards from the Queen Mother who was up on a big daïs. Dead silence. Live TV all around the world.

There was a party afterwards at St James' Palace. The Queen Mother is a remarkable lady. She always says the right thing, unlike the rest of us. After a couple drinks, I was chatting away and I said, 'Ma'am, did you enjoy your birthday party?' and she said, 'Oh, Sir John, I did. It was wonderful…and you made it you know.' What a thing to say.

Me 1983 'Little Lies' Wyndham's Theatre

There was a play called *The Magistrate* by Sir Arthur Wing Pinero and it's played quite a large part in my life. First of all in a picture called *Those Were the Days* in 1934 with Will Hay starring as the Magistrate and me as the boy. Then I put it into my one-man show. But before that, an American sent me a version of *The Magistrate* called *Little Lies*. I was horrified at first because *The Magistrate* is a classic but the script was funny and it presented me with a remarkable opportunity to be outrageous. The play ran at Wyndham's for a long time and was quite a big success.

Me, Helen Hayes and Bette Davis 1985, 'Murder with Mirrors'

I've had one or two disappointments during what I laughingly call 'my career'. One of the big ones was to do with a film called *The African Queen*. I had signed with Rank to produce, direct and act and I went out to find stories. I found *The African Queen* and thought it was terrific and wanted to buy it. Unfortunately Arthur Rank was away and, by the time he was back in the office it had been sold, for $50,000. The part that Bogey played brilliantly was an English Cockney, perfect for me. I had given the book to Bette, who adored it. But there were are…

Me and Melissa *1984, California*

Mary and John Gielgud *1985*

Lovely shot of Mary and Johnny G in his wonderful garden.

Mary and Judi Dench *1985, London*

Many years ago Ralph Richardson said, 'It's been suggested, Johnnie, that you take over from me as president of Mountview Theatre School.' And I said, ' Well, Ralph, I'm very flattered and would love to follow in your footsteps but actually I have a couple of pictures laid on and a play and I have to tell you…'Good,' he said, 'I knew you would be good at it…' And put the phone down! The next thing I know I have the Chief Executive, Peter Coxhead of Mountview, ringing up and saying, 'We're delighted you're going to be president.' And I still am. This is a picture of Judi, who went to Mountview and passed out with a top diploma.

Me, Queen Elizabeth, David Frost and Jerry Lewis *1986*

The first time I met the Queen was at a garden party at Buckingham Palace when she and Princes Margaret were very young.

Joan Plowright *1985 (left)*

Me and Madonna *1987, 'Who's that Girl?', Hollywood*

A lot of people asked why I was making a picture with Madonna and I said, for two reasons. First is money and secondly I have seen her work and I admire and like her.

  We were in Hollywood filming and the director, who was very young, fell, quite naturally, madly in love with Madonna and I think that is why the picture wasn't the hit it should have been because he couldn't bear to cut away from Madonna. It was a comedy and he couldn't bear to leave her and everybody knows that you have to cut away and get laughs on another face. But she was charming and very professional and nice to work with.

Me and Lionel Jeffries

1987, 'Pygmalion', New York

Although Peter O'Toole was terribly sick during the run, drinking gallons of water and smoking 40 cigarettes a day, he did still manage to turn in a brilliant performance.

It was also wonderful to work with my old friend Lionel.

I played Dolittle and thoroughly enjoyed myself, although I couldn't help expecting some musical numbers.

Me *1987, 'Tale of Two Cities' (opposite)*

Me And Mary *1982, Hills House Denham*
Me and my Polaroid.

We started our 'sign-in books' during the 60s. In 1982 Mary had the idea of taking a Polaroid shot at the same time and sticking it next to our guests' signatures and comment. Here are a just a few of these memories.

Dickie and Sheila Attenborough *(top)*

Hayley, Crispian, Ace, Dickie and Sheila *(bottom)*

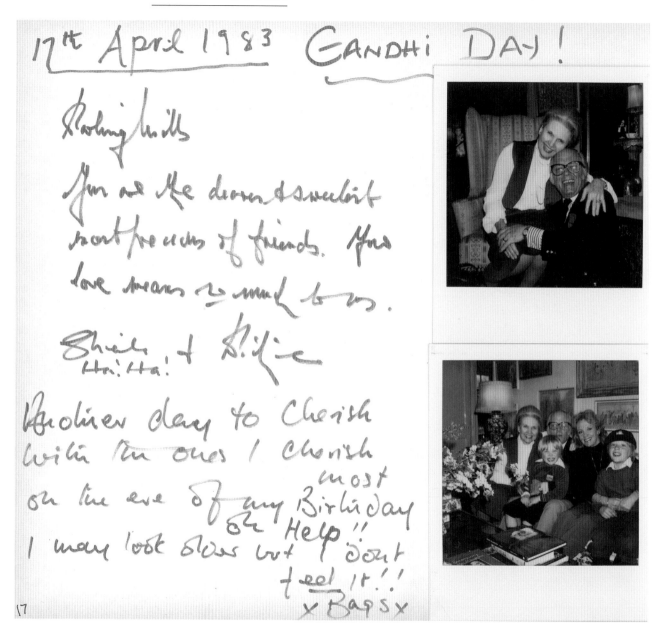

17th April 1983   GANDHI DAY!

186

Nov. 14th 1982.

Crispian
ACe
and Bagwash
for my darlings xxxxx
Bless you both forever 💕→
I love you so much x

Xmas 1982

Jany 22nd 1983. Mary's Birthday.

Rosie xx + Donald. 22/1/83.

Ken & Nem. Maxwell ms.
Birthday Party
22.1.83.

Hayley, Crispian and Ace

Sep 9th '84. Sir DAVID & Lady Lean Day.

Lovely to see you both again my dears!
David & Sandy

My dears, What a lovely celebration! The
champagne was divine. And I shall never
ever forget that magnificent Talbot '66 !!
Your most affectionate
Sandy

David and Sandy Lean *just after David was knighted.*

July 8ᵗʰ '84

Jim – love, darling friends.... and a huge THANK you... x Tony (Q) & Dot

Tony and Dot Quayle

July 14ᵗʰ '84

May God's blessing be with you always. My love. *Cushing*

Thank you both for a lovely evening Love, Gillian

Thank you Watson We'll get you in the end! MORIARTY (a.k.a. Kevin FRANCIS)

Kevin Francis, Gillian and Peter Cushing

V.I.P. DAY !!   Nov 18th '84.

Bette Davis
Helen Hayes
such joy

Great company +
marvelous hostes -
thank you for having
me into your home.
Dick Lamp

Dulcie Gray, Allan Davis, Bette Davis, Helen Hayes.

Sep 8th '85.

Darling Johnnie (David Bailey eat your
heart out) and Mary — What a
lot we are! Still we're all here!!
Love and ×× Nanette ××

& love from the eccentric writer

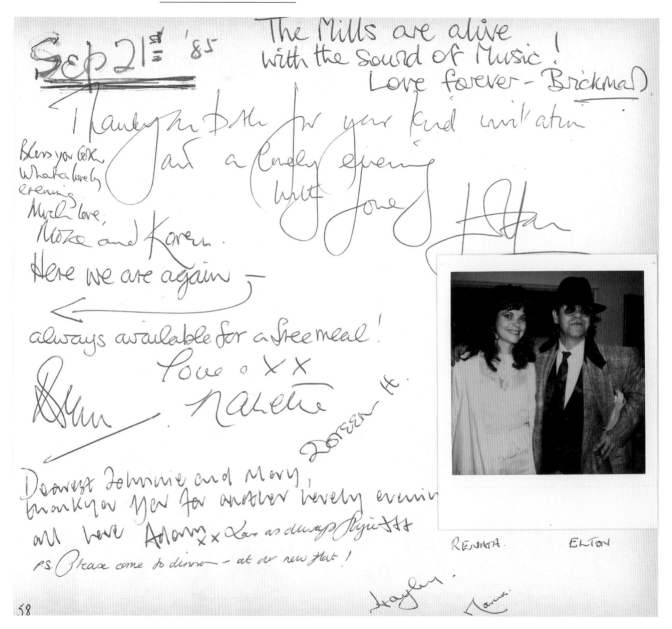

Sep 21ˢᵗ '85

The Mills are alive
with the sound of Music!
Love forever - Brickman

Thank you both for your kind invitation
and a lovely evening

Bless you Coke
What a lovely
evening

Much love,
Moke and Karen.

Here we are again —

always available for a free meal!
Love ° XX
Nalene

Dearest Johnnie and Mary,
thank you for another lovely evening
all love Adam
P.S. Please come to dinner – at our new flat!

58

RENATA.   ELTON

Elton John and Renata, *1985*

Elton came to dinner at Hills House
one evening with his wife, Renata, and
we had a marvellous evening.

I must say I thought Elton's
performance at Princess Diana's
memorial service was stunning. It was
a terribly emotional occasion, and
somehow Elton got through his
moving tribute without breaking
down.

June 7th 1988.

Love and Kisses
my darlings —
Mary.

and LOL.

June 16th..

What a lovely
surprise to see ya
both & ya wonderful
home. a Welcome
relief after a few
"Tears in the Rain"!

All Love

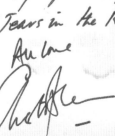

Pippa, Catherine and Shirley, 1980

Tony and Dorothy Quayle 1980

Leslie and Evie Bricusse, 1980

Molly (Bud) Blake 1980

Laurence and Mary Evans *(opposite top)*
Laurence has been a wonderful agent for almost half a century. Without him I wouldn't have had half the success I've had, and without him I would be 10% richer.

Christopher Cazenove *(opposite bottom)*

Jonathan and Vincent Price *1979*

Donald and Rosie Chilvers and Hugh Stewart*1980*

Three of my greatest friends. Donald Chilvers was one of Cooper Lybrand's whiz-kids, retired now and busier than ever.

Jack Lemmon, Doreen Hawkins, Kevin Spacey, me and Marg, *1986.*
Jack Lemmon is probably the greatest comic actor in the business, and not bad on the piano either.

THE 1990s

Me, Lionel Jeffries, Michael Hordern, Wendy Hiller, Googie Withers and Kingsley Amis *1990, 'Ending Up'*
A marvellous Kingsley Amis story that was made into a TV movie. We shot it on Ian Fleming's country estate.

Me, Spike Milligan and Eric Sykes 1992

I was invited to dinner one night by Barry Humphries, who is probably better known as Dame Edna Everage. He said, 'We're having a small dinner party . . . we've got Spike Milligan, Eric Sykes, Billy Connolly and Harry Secombe. The guest of honour is Prince Charles. It's just after this ghastly skiing tragedy which has upset him badly, so we thought we'd invite him along and have a few laughs because, as you know, he loved The Goons and I'm sure he'd love to see you.' I couldn't see the logic but I set off for his house in Hampstead, and we had a driver who thought he was in Bristol and totally lost his way. Then a message came through that the prince unfortunately was not going to be there. We were nearly an hour late. I dashed up the steps, tripped up and landed on the carpet on my face. When I got up, there was Prince Charles facing me. He had come to the party in the end. It was the start of a very memorable evening. Gales of laughter.

Me and Princess Diana 1992 *London*

One of the many charity dinners that I attended was at the Hilton. The guest of honour was Princess Diana, who was looking her radiant best. Mary and I were at the top table and Mary was about ten places away from me. Now, being a sentimentalist, if I wasn't sitting next to my wife, I always used to send a note down the table saying, 'Darling, did I remember to tell you that I love you?' So on this occasion I wrote this note and said to the headwaiter, 'Give this to the very attractive lady down there with the golden hair.' So I'm getting on with my dinner and suddenly look up and there he is handing the note to Princess Diana.

Me in My One Man Show
1993, Australia

I opened my one-man show at Watford, which went down very well. This shot is from the Australian tour in 1993 where I went with Mary and Johnny. A very successful six-city tour.

Left: **Roy Castle** *1994*
Above: **Me, Fiona Castle and Cliff Richard**

Roy Castle was one of the most courageous men I have ever met in my life. This picture (left) was taken at the launching of the Roy Castle Fund for Lung Cancer Research. We met at Paddington station at 7.30 in the morning and he was desperately ill. We toured around the station on a luggage cart doing interviews, then we boarded the train, and did some more interviews. From time to time Roy had to be given injections by his wife, Fiona.

We arrived in Liverpool and he went straight to bed. That evening we were doing the show at the Empire Theatre. Roy was looking simply ghastly. He could hardly walk, and he was due to go on stage and make a big appeal. Three minutes before his cue, his legs stopped shaking, he had one last injection and went out and did twelve minutes, flat out. The only thing he said he couldn't do was play his trumpet. I have never seen such a terrific, brave performance and nobody would have known there was anything wrong with him at all. A few weeks later, of course, he died. His wife, Fiona, was wonderful and, as you may know, the fund has now reached over £10m.

Me and Andrew Lloyd Webber *1997*

We went to see an amateur production of *Whistle Down the Wind* in Edinburgh. It was extremely good and we had a very entertaining evening. When we got back home, I turned to Mary and said, ' I've got to call somebody up about this show.' So I called Andrew Lloyd Webber, whom I had only met a couple of times. I told him we had seen a musical of *Whistle Down the Wind* which is Mary's story and he said he had heard of it. I said, 'Honestly Andrew, you just have to get up and see it.' He said, 'I'd love to, really, but I can't, we're having another baby.' I said, ' You can have another baby but you won't get another chance to see this because it is the last performance tomorrow.' So he took the shuttle, caught the last performance on the Saturday night, bought the book, wrote new music, put it on, and the show's still running in London and it is a big success.

Me and Paul Scofield *1995*
'Martin Chuzzlewit' BBC

I had not done a Dickens since *Great Expectations*, and to my joy I was offered the part of Mr. Chuffey in *Martin Chuzzlewit*. The big attraction to me was not only was it a good part in a BBC production but that it also gave me the chance to play opposite a man I had admired for many years, Paul Scofield. I played *Ross* in New York when he was doing *A Man for All Seasons* there and we got to know each other quite well. He's a very secret man, and after we had renewed our acquaintance, we were talking quite freely and in the middle of dinner one night I came out with a quick right hander. I said, 'Paul, did you turn down a knighthood?' He paused with spoon in mid air and said, 'Say that again.' So I said, 'Why did you turn down a knighthood?' He thought for a minute and said, 'Why don't I like meringues?' I knew what he meant so I didn't press the point. Then he said, 'Well actually, I'll tell you, I think I still prefer being called Mr. Scofield.'

Me and John Novelli *1998, Buckingham Palace*

This picture was taken at Buckingham Palace at the Not Forgotten Society Garden Party. It was a wonderful affair. Everything was very relaxed and cameras were allowed in. I'm standing with an amazing character called John Francisco Novelli, my manager, who, in a very short space of time, has become a very good friend of the family. I spent two hours with the chaps and knew many of them. Even a survivor of 'The Kelly' was there. At five-to-five, I said to John, 'That's it, I really have to go now,' when a lady about 85 came rushing up saying, 'Oh, just one minute, just one more picture, could you please, just one more…' And I said, 'Yes, of course.' So she clicked and said, 'Oh, that is kind of you, so nice to meet you, but, who are you?'

Crispian and Kula Shaker *1996*

Crispian started the band Kula Shaker in 1996. Their first album went to number one on the charts. It was very exciting for me when I went to see him play at the Astoria. A huge and well deserved success.

Me, Mary Eric Sykes and Bob Hoskins *1997, 'The Big Freeze', Finland*

I'd been a fan of Eric Sykes for many years. He is one of the great English comedians, a man of enormous charm. So I was delighted when he rang me up saying, 'Johnnie, I want you to come up and make one of my comedies with me.' I said I would love to. 'OK,' he said, 'I'll just talk to your agent and everything and get it fixed up.' I said, 'Fine, get the script over here and I'll give you an answer right away.' 'What script?' he said. I said, 'The film script.'

He said he didn't have a script. 'You know I cannot see much or hear now but it is all in my head. I know what the story is but I don't have a synopsis and I change it a lot.' I said I wasn't going to tell my agent that. 'Why don't you say I've got a script and like it?' So that's what he did. I took the plane with Mary to Helsinki with not a clue what I was doing. He said, 'It's a very good part for you.' Maybe it was. Eric made it up as he went along.

Me and Mary *1997, Finland*

Me *1998, 'Cats'*

In the summer of 1998, Andrew Lloyd Webber called me to ask, 'Johnnie, will you play Gus, the old theatre cat in *Cats*? I'm shooting the video. It would only take you a few days. I said, 'Well, it sounds rather exciting. I haven't seen the show for seventeen years; I was there on the first night. Can you get me a couple of tickets?' Believe it or not, he could only get the house seats. I went to see the show again and, of course, I fell hook, line and sinker for it. I had two or three rehearsals with Gillian Lynne, the brilliant choreographer who started the show off, and the musical director. We shot it on the stage of the Adelphi where in 1932 I did *Words and Music*, the Noel Coward Review, and the place was full of ghosts. It was a strange and rather marvellous experience. Terrific make-up, which took about an hour and a half. I went down on the stage and the director, David Mallet, said, 'It's great make-up, now I suggest you go upstairs and get yourself aged-up a bit.' Which I thought was rather funny, since I was ninety years old.

Me, Mary, Juliet, Hayley, Jonathan, and Andrew Lloyd Webber
1998, The very special first night of 'Whistle Down the Wind'

The first night of *Whistle Down the Wind* at the Aldwych was quite an occasion. Andrew got us the Royal Box and we had Mary there, who was on very good form that night.

Me, Judi Dench, Michael Williams, Nanette Newman, Anthony Andrews, Leslie and Evie Bricusse and Andrew Lloyd Webber *1998*
90th birthday party given by The Greater London Fund for the Blind at the Dorchester Hotel

Henry and Melissa *1999, Sherman Oaks, California*

Henry is in college in Hawaii now studying Marine Biology and Melissa is an actress and artist.

Me and Tony Blair *1998*

This is an extraordinary picture of me with the Prime Minister, Tony Blair. Since I can remember I've voted Conservative. I'm not really into politics like Dickie Attenborough, although I'm vaguely interested when I'm not working. But I have to tell you that at this last election I voted for Tony Blair. The still was taken at 10 Downing Street for the Greater London Fund for the Blind, of which I am the President.

Henry Mills *1995, Hawaii*

In 1995 Henry went on the ASP World Surfing Tour. Thirty contests a year in twenty different countries.

Michael Caine *1999*

Mary and I went to see the premiere of *Zulu* with a marvellous performance by a young actor I had never heard of called Michael Caine. At the party afterwards Mary and I had a chat with him. I said 'It's a damn good picture and if I may say so, you gave a splendid performance.' He smiled and in very broad Cockney replied, 'Yeah, well, thanks very much, mate, was a good one wasn't it.' In the film Michael had played an English aristocrat. He is the only actor I know who could have got away with it.

Juliet *1999, 'Passions', Hollywood*

A still from Juliet's new NBC series *Passions*, in which she has been enormously successful. A fabulous character part for her.

Hayley and Roddy McDowall *1998*
Roddy was a dear man and a great friend of the family.

Juliet and Melissa
1998, 'Blithe Spirit'

This is a picture of Juliet and my granddaughter, Melissa, who made her debut in *Blithe Spirit* playing the maid. Noel wrote marvellous parts for maids and Melissa really was excellent. From that moment I feared she was doomed for a life in the theatre.

Me and Stephen Fry

1999, Hills House

The first real time I met Stephen Fry was on my eighty-fifth birthday. A lot of people came to my party at Hills House. Stephen arrived and put a package on the hall table with the other presents, and I thanked him. We had a very good party and, as always, the actors were the last to leave. Stephen was the very last. On the way out, he said, 'Would you like to open your present now?' I thought it would be a bottle of something, but I opened the bag and it was Noel Coward's dressing gown, the one I'd seen him play *Private Lives* in, back in 1930. I couldn't believe it. It had been in an auction of his memorabilia and Stephen must have paid a packet for it. It was such a thoughtful thing to do. Noel was the single most important person in my career. Anyway, Stephen asked what I was going to do with it and I said I was going to put it in a glass case. Right now it is hanging on the back of the loo door! In these stills, taken by Johnny and me in February, Stephen is wearing the dressing gown, a most appropriate person to be wearing it.

Me *1999, Hills House, Denham*